298
02

DATE LOANED

GAYLORD 3563

PRINTED IN U.S.A.

The Art of W. C. Fields

The Art of W. C. Fields

by William K. Everson

BONANZA BOOKS · NEW YORK

Acknowledgments

Grateful acknowledgment is extended to the following individuals for their help in supplying rare stills from their own collections:

John E. Allen
Carlos Clarens
Alex Gordon
Gerald D. McDonald
Andrew C. McKay
Rudolph Stone

I wish also to thank the following organizations for their cooperation:

The D. W. Griffith Estate
MCA
Metro-Goldwyn-Mayer
Paramount Pictures
United Artists
Universal Pictures

Special acknowledgment is extended to Raymond Rohauer for the use of certain stills from his film properties.

Dedicated to my wife, Sandy, who successfully guided two children through the Baby LeRoy stage without (yet) going through a Kathleen Howard stage herself.

Contents

The Art of W. C. Fields

1.

W. C. Fields-
The Image and the Man

Charlie Chaplin was "Everyman" in the guise of a lovable little tramp. William S. Hart was the strong silent Western hero who usually died at the end of his films protecting the girl he loved.

These are the kind of facile generalizations that continually are offered in an effort to file away the great movie personalities of the past conveniently wrapped up in little niches. Both of the above examples have been quoted *ad nauseam*, and, far from even approximating the truth, both are gross distortions. Chaplin, whatever he may have been, was no "Everyman," and was much too aggressive to be lovable. William S. Hart had nobility all right, but he died only once or twice in his films, and was too much of a sentimentalist to pass up winning the girl in time for a happy fadeout.

Perhaps more than any other screen personality, W. C. Fields has suffered from this over-simplification of his screen character. His anti-social attitudes— perhaps because they are the most fun and provide the best copy—have been seized

1

upon gleefully, as though they were the whole of his characterization. Yet in point of fact, Fields was a sympathetic underdog on the screen far more than he was a conniving charlatan. Hatred of dogs and children, distrust of bankers and foreigners, may have been ingrained traits, but in his films, at least, they were in some way justified by circumstances.

Off-screen, Fields was far more complex than he appeared to be in his films, his obstinacies, irrational quirks, foibles and sudden switches of mood (generosity became miserliness overnight; friends were changed into grasping enemies and back to friends again without ever knowing of the metamorphosis) making him hard to get along with, even for his best friends. Those who loved and knew him best were constantly being infuriated by him and forever on the verge of renouncing him, while those who knew him only casually often gave him up as a bad job. Despite the wicked and puckish sense of humor which ruled his whole life, he was not a "lovable eccentric" off-screen. He was neither poseur nor hypocrite. Both on-screen image and off-screen man were honest and interchangeable extensions of the same individual, something extremely rare among movie personalities in general, and comedians in particular.

Even more so than Chaplin, Fields could claim that his early years of extreme hardship helped shape him as a comedian. Both Chaplin and Fields grew up as Dickensian Oliver Twists, suffering more than their share of hunger, poverty and hard knocks. But when in their later years of affluence they called on their youth for film material and inspiration, their paths diverged. Chaplin remained Oliver Twist, continuing to "ask for more" in terms of audience approval, understanding and sympathy, often incorporating biographical material into his films through a combination of nostalgia and self-pity. Fields wiped the slate clean by hitting back; he purged himself of those hard years by making fun of them, or by ridiculing the kind of people who had helped to make those years so difficult. Since there never was any hint of self-pity in his work, it was almost as though he were using the resources of a major studio to make a series of expensive home movies. They were movies made for himself rather than for audiences, although audiences laughed at them too much to know that, or to care.

Born William Claude Dukenfield in or around 1879—the exact date has never been confirmed—Fields was one of five children of a Cockney immigrant father and an American mother. In later years Fields was to profess himself extremely proud of his British heritage, and to put it forward as a logical reason for being given straight dramatic roles (especially Dickensian ones) instead of exclusively comic material.

The family was poor, and Fields got but sparse schooling in between spells of working for his father, a fruit and vegetable peddler. Fields ran away from home at the age of eleven, after having been hit even harder than usual in a running argument with his father. The years that followed were bad; Fields knew hunger, cold, and the inside of jails. He frequently had to steal to survive. Constant exposure to the elements affected his voice, which took on the rasping quality that would stay with him for the rest of his life. Another trademark acquired during this period was the large bulbous nose, the result of a beating rather than a youthful devotion to liquor, although Fields' well-known fondness for the bottle undoubtedly did much to preserve it in all its colorful, contoured glory.

Through these incredibly lean years, Fields not only survived but even managed to save money, learning a respect for frugality and security which was to leap to epic proportions in later years. Ever afraid of some unlikely Doomsday when all avenues of work might be closed to him, he developed a mania for opening bank accounts wherever he went, here and abroad, in metropolis and hamlet. It has been estimated that at the peak of his provisions for future rainy days, he maintained in excess of seven hundred bank accounts, many of them presumably under tongue-twisting fictional names, so that they still lie gathering dust and interest in sleepy little towns where Fields passed but once.

By the time he was fourteen years old, he had made himself into an adept amateur juggler, and entered show business by one of the traditional routes of the day—taking menial jobs in fairs and circuses where he got occasional chances to display his juggling skill between such chores as driving tent pegs and carrying water. During these years he had his first encounters with that breed of rascal whom he was to play so often in later movies—the road show manager who absconds with all the funds, leaving his cast and crew stranded and penniless. Carefully and laboriously—though his progress from water-boy to fledgling theatrical performer was accomplished in a mere eight years—the entirely self-taught and self-disciplined Fields worked his way out of the tent shows into vaudeville where he was earning one hundred and twenty-five dollars a week. At the turn of the century, when only twenty, he went on vaudeville tours to Europe, sharing bills with such local headliners as Maurice Chevalier. Plays followed vaudeville, and Fields' stature grew steadily. In 1915, he was signed for "The Ziegfeld Follies." He was now earning two hundred dollars a week, and was so sure of himself that already he was beginning the first of a lifetime series of arguments with managers and directors who had the temerity to dispute his concepts of comedy. 1915 too saw his first appearance in movies, in the short comedy "Pool Sharks," and from this point on there was no stopping him.

In the final analysis, all that really matters about an artist is his work—the printed word in a book, the notations of the music in the score, the paint on the canvas or, in Fields' case, the image on the screen. Success or failure can and should be judged solely by the end result, and the sympathy one automatically feels for a man who suffered as much as Fields in his earlier days has to be ruthlessly pushed aside. If the work is good, the fact that it draws its roots and inspirations from the creator's own life is both incidental and unimportant. If the work fails, the added consideration that it is partly autobiographical, or that the author was trying to make a statement, is an irrelevant rationalization. (It is this rationalization that has sustained many of the weaker Chaplin films beyond their true worth.)

If comedy is to be both enjoyed and appraised honestly, it has to be approached from a point of view of consistency. Buster Keaton, Harry Langdon, Laurel and Hardy all were extremely funny and creative comedians, but none of their films were in any way autobiographical. They were not trying to make personal statements, other than comic and satiric ones, and to them film was merely the best medium in which to be funny and reach the widest audience. Thus to search for motivation in Chaplin and Fields films, while regarding Keaton and Langdon on the more superficial level of merely whether they are funny or not, creates an unfair and pointless division. Obviously Fields' films are full of personal quirks and attitudes toward life, but the films themselves tell us this; and, more importantly, the films would work purely as comedies even if we didn't know that Fields the comic and Fields the man are inseparable and that he was ticking off a lot of old scores.

Fields' oft-stated hatred for dogs and children, despite the knowledge of the publicity-wise that such statements made good copy, was genuine enough. Understandably, he didn't choose to feel sentimental about those years of his life when the friendship of other children and the companionship of a dog—all a part of growing up for most youngsters—were denied him. This deliberate rejection of sentiment was to be one of the springboards of his comedy style, but always his hostility and aggression had to be justified, if not condoned. Fields invariably approached babies on the screen warily, but prepared to meet them half-way. Of course his good-natured confidence in their ability to meet him half-way was misplaced.

Seeing a baby with a loose diaper pin in "The Barber Shop," he is all paternal concern. "Let me get that, little Woolly Britches," he coos soothingly. "A thing like that could kill you!" As he bends over to retrieve the loose pin, the baby belts his undefended head with a full bottle of milk. Stalking away, rubbing his injured head, he sees to it that the over-sized pin, its sharp point deliberately and murderously exposed, is left where the baby's eagerly exploring fingers will find it quickly. His notorious feuds with child star Baby LeRoy are legendary, and Hollywood never tires of recalling the time when Fields, irked by LeRoy's unwitting scene-stealing, deliberately got the hard-working and obedient child drunk by spiking his orange juice with hard liquor, having first disposed of a watchful nurse by pretending tender solicitude for the "little nipper." With the young star, happy and healthy a moment before, suddenly in a drunken stupor, the hapless director was at a loss. "Walk him around," suggested Fields, an old hand at dealing with drunks, and then triumphantly bellowed, "Send him home! The kid's no trouper!"

The Fields-LeRoy exchanges in his films of the thirties were delightful essays in malicious sadism, though Fields was the victim as often as he was the tormentor. Privately, he seemed to hold considerable affection for the youngster, and was known to go out of his way to be nice to him in a paternal way, buying him many presents, and in a business way too, writing extraneous roles for the child into his own scripts at times when LeRoy's fortunes seemed to be ebbing.

Dogs and children apart, Fields' list of personal antipathies was a long one, distinguished by a distrust of bankers from president down to humble teller, a conviction that policemen used their powers of authority only to persecute the innocent, and an instinctive hostile reaction toward foreigners and Negroes.* Without much geographic or ancestral justification, he constantly referred to his good friend, American-born director Gregory La Cava, as "that dago son-of-a-bitch," considered all Orientals as minions of Fu Manchu, and frequently reacted in shock and horror when it was contrived in his own movie scripts to have Negroes appear stealthily, if innocently, from behind him. Delicately avoiding obvious racial slurs in his scripts, he frequently had recourse to the phrase, "There's an Ethiopian in the fuel supply," when something went badly astray. "Who's the Chief Ubangi around here?" he asks in "You Can't Cheat an Honest Man," addressing Eddie "Rochester" Anderson, who plays the leader of a group of lazy, shiftless, crap-shooting Negro stereotypes.

Yet if one can trace these and other personal resentments to events in his own life, how does one explain his richest and in some ways most acutely observed comedy set-piece—the horrifying "average" American family? In "It's a Gift," "The Man on the Flying Trapeze," "The Bank Dick" and other films, Fields presents hilarious and uncomfortably convincing portraits of a humble, hard-working, well-meaning husband, hemmed in on all sides by obnoxious brats of children, Amazonian wives who nag him all night and serve him cold toast for breakfast, vicious and critical mothers-in-law and fat, lazy, sponging relatives—topped off by noisy and gossiping neighbors.

There seems nothing in Fields' life on which to base this year-in, year-out indictment of The American Family. The hardship of Fields' own early family life was brought on by poverty rather than incompatibility; Fields loved his mother and his brothers and, as soon as he was able, began to send money home to them regularly. He married at the turn of the century, while still a very young man, and for many years the marriage was a happy one, with Fields as devoted to his in-laws as to his own family. Never anything but the master of his own destiny and the head of his household, even if his home was usually a hotel room, he was certainly the very antithesis of a nagged, henpecked, down-trodden husband. He might conceivably have harbored some kind of grudge against his father, but it is more likely that he understood that it was the desperateness of their straits that led to the ultimate beating which caused Fields to leave home. Interestingly enough, while in his scripts Fields created movie families that were overrun with nagging wives and mothers

* In view of the exaggerated emphasis that may be placed on Fields' apparent aversion to Negroes in these race-conscious Civil Rights days, it should be pointed out that this was merely one of Fields' mile-long list of pet peeves. There was never a deeply felt conviction about, or underlying reason for, any of Fields' purely superficial prejudices, many of which were probably caused by isolated incidents or even mere suspicion. The many gags about Negroes in his films were generally of a genial nature, and established that whatever he felt about Negroes, he held them in considerably higher esteem than doctors and bank officials. He is known to have been generous with his own Negro staff, and on at least one occasion when they were spoken to disparagingly by a visiting friend of his, the friend was ordered out of the house.

and selfish, unappreciative children, they have *never* included a father, unsympathetic or otherwise. (Fields usually played a father, of course, but he never provided himself with a screen father as a butt for jokes or personal recriminations.)

Divorced from all his sight gags, props and routines, Fields was quite probably the funniest single individual America has ever produced. Yet the character he created for the screen was spectacularly lacking in most of the elements of "popular appeal" then considered essential for a screen comedian. All of the leading comedians—and their work and styles seldom overlapped—had strongly individual traits. Chaplin, despite the aggression in much of his work and the fact that most of his movie problems were of his own making, did suggest that there was a latent nobility in man. Harold Lloyd was the epitome of the go-getting American, brash, anxious to prove himself, willing to turn any situation to his own advantage, but nevertheless a firm believer in honesty as the best policy, and unwilling to accept success at a compromise of those ideals. Buster Keaton was a pessimist, a visitor from another world, stumbling about this planet as if in a dream, and overcoming hostility and obstacles by bringing to them his own peculiar and other-worldly logic. Unsentimental and dry, he was the least popular of the major comedians, and the cleverest. Harry Langdon, whose vogue was brief, was literally, in dress, behavior and attitudes, a baby and, like all babies, cunning and sometimes malicious despite his innocence.

In one way or another, all these men lived in little worlds unique unto themselves. Fields, on the other hand, was very much of this world, usually trapped by it, and fighting back gamely if futilely. In the last reel his worm usually turned and made the family fortune, but this was more a form of wish-fulfillment than anything else. His climaxes rarely had even the limited logic or probability of the Keaton, Lloyd or Langdon happy endings or the wistful Chaplin finish. In one other key sense, too, he differed from them. All four—indeed the majority of screen comedians—made it a point to be in one way or another inferior to their audiences, in terms of either ability, social standing, intelligence or physical appearance.

Audiences automatically warmed to a character they could feel mildly sorry for, and they never have shown the same warmth or affection for those other and more recent comedians who have adopted a superior, smart alecky stance and condescendingly played down to their audience. (Most of these have come from radio or nightclubs, where the stress has been on smart patter, and the emotional rapport with the audience is of less immediate importance.) Fields, on the other hand, made himself neither a figure of humility nor one of superiority. He met his audiences head on, on an equal level, and in the prohibition and depression eras of the twenties and thirties, when the nobility of Chaplin or the integrity of Lloyd seemed a trifle unrealistic, the direct honesty of Fields worked. Audiences might not exactly identify with him—not wanting to admit either to a depressed family or business status or, on the other hand, to sharing in such a larcenous makeup—but they certainly could recognize and relate to Fields on their own level.

Just as the comedians varied in their approach to getting ahead in life, so did they offer divergent approaches to women, love and sex. Chaplin exploited his role of gallant protector to earn a cloak of honor and nobility for his basically self-centered little tramp. To Lloyd, winning the love of his girl was merely another symbol of success. His love was honest and genuine, but one suspected that his marriages were as chaste as his climbs to affluence had been pure. Langdon, the baby and near-innocent, knew just enough about girls and sex to be afraid of them, while Keaton, so totally divorced from the affairs of this world, was never able to understand that his heroines were too dull and stupid to be worth the effort he expended on them.

The last scene of Keaton's 1924 classic "Sherlock Junior" perfectly sums up his relationship with the opposite sex. Finally reunited with his fiancee, he can no longer escape the responsibilities of love and marriage. Fortunately, the reunion takes place in a movie theatre, and he can be guided by the lovers on the screen. As the hero places a ring on the girl's finger, Keaton studies the scene intently, and then places a ring on *his* girl's finger. The preliminary screen embrace is likewise studied and then copied by Keaton; so is the follow-up kiss, though by now he is more cautious and restrained in his imitation. The final image in the movie within a movie is of a passionate embrace, which dissolves, establishes a time lapse, and fades back in again to show hero and heroine now happily married, the husband bouncing twin children on his knee. This is entirely beyond Keaton's ken. What on earth has happened? He scratches his head in forlorn puzzlement and frustration as "Sherlock Junior" abandons him, high and dry, the "End" title leaving his predicament unsolved.

Fields' approach to women was to regard most of them as enemies and busybodies; his attitude toward sex was to ignore it. In most of his films he is already past the romantic age, his only interest in girls a paternal one. His grown-up daughters (Mary Brian and others) were beautiful and loving, serving as counterpoint to his aggressive wives and providing such romantic sub-plots as were thought necessary in his films. Only in "My Little Chickadee" did Fields begin to think seriously—and longingly—about sex. But alas! his fake marriage to Mae West was never consummated, and his wedding night joined the golf and pool routines as yet another essay in frustration.

Unlike that of the other great screen comedians, who all were imitated either blatantly or covertly by lesser talents, Fields' sense of humor was so bizarre and so uniquely tied up with his own personality that none of his competitors ever tried to emulate him.* Instead he provided endless fodder for the radio impersonators (not even Edward G. Robinson's snarling gangster lingo was so frequently imitated as Fields' "My Little Chickadee" and other catch-phrases), while the Fieldsian figure itself frequently turned up in caricature in the animated cartoons of the thirties, in unflattering portraits that tended to over-emphasize his large nose and drinking propensities.

*   An exception to this was the case of Will Hay, a former music hall performer who became the leading British screen comic of the thirties. His work often included a rather curious amalgam of the story-lines of Keaton with the personal characteristics of Fields.

One of the richest and most affectionate portraits of Fields as a man is to be found in Robert Lewis Taylor's admirable biography, W. C. *Fields, His Follies and Fortunes* (Doubleday, 1949). It is that rare thing, a book about a funny man that is funny in itself. However, it proves once again that celebrities and their friends are often their own worst historians; direct quotes from Fields, La Cava, Gene Fowler and others of the Fieldsian coterie display an incredible lack of regard for the actualities—so notably that one is not tempted to delve too far into the reliability of many of the marvelous anecdotes.

It is hardly likely for example that Fields, during his period at the Long Island Paramount studio, would have demanded a salary commensurate with those paid to Valentino and Wallace Reid. Reid had died several years earlier, and Valentino, who had left Paramount earlier, also died the same year that Fields went to work for Paramount. Fields' own accounts of working with Mack Sennett's Keystone outfit imply that he was with Sennett during his heyday rather than in his final producing years. Fields made four well-disciplined two-reelers for Sennett, not one of which contained a single lion or even a lion cub, thus deflating his meticulously detailed account of being chased by a lion for a lengthy routine in a Sennett movie. Even so well-known a film as "My Man Godfrey" is somehow worked into an anecdote which requires it to have been made at Paramount in 1934, whereas it was made at Universal in 1936. But we need not cavil. It is one of the rules of the game that actors' reminiscences are not to be taken literally, and the Fieldsian flights of fancy are quite mild compared to some of the tall tales that Mae West spun in her autobiography, fondly assuming no doubt that her movies would not be seen again to hoist her by her own petard.

Fortunately movies do survive and endure, sustaining legends and sometimes obliterating them. Even if Fields had never had a biographer to record his diatribes and anecdotes, his films would more than do the job of keeping his legend alive.

Fields displays his juggling dexterity in "*Poppy.*" (Courtesy of Paramount Pictures)

☞ 2.

The Lost Films

In the course of a film career that began in 1915 and spanned some thirty years, W. C. Fields appeared in, frequently wrote and sometimes unofficially directed a total of forty-two films. Of these, twelve have either vanished from the face of the earth or are otherwise unavailable. It is an optimistic distortion, however, to say that seventy-five percent of his screen work remains for our enjoyment and reappraisal, because the existing films include his six short subjects, and seven features in which his participation was limited to specific segments or brief guest roles.

Conversely, the missing twenty-five percent consists of almost his entire output from the formative silent years, of which only two representative films (including, happily, his first) are today known to exist. No other major screen comedian has such a gigantic gap in the preserved record of his work, and certainly no other comedian is so lacking in films to illustrate the creation and development of a screen character.

Chaplin's work is almost entirely preserved and reasonably accessible, despite the great number of early and confusingly similar shorts that he made before he hit his stride. Thanks to film archives throughout the world, a handful of collectors and the stars themselves, the careers of Harold Lloyd, Buster Keaton and Harry Langdon are singularly well documented. Out of approximately one hundred Laurel and Hardy subjects, only two or three have disappeared, and we have further evidence of the development of their individual comedy styles from many examples of their separate film work prior to their teaming.

But with Fields the outlook is discouraging; if at this late date more of his silents are to be re-discovered, it will be due more to luck and accident than to organized search through the usual channels. Fields' case parallels that of John Ford, one of our major American directors, whose approximately sixty silent films are represented by only some three or four survivors, making a detailed study of his entire career quite impossible. Fortunately, the films of our greatest director, D. W. Griffith, have been largely preserved. Only two or three of his films seem to have been lost, and these are not major ones. But how little of the whole structure of film history would we know if Griffith were represented today only by one of his early one-reelers, and perhaps "Way Down East," with "The Birth of a Nation," "Intolerance," "Broken Blossoms" and all the rest being merely names in reference books. How impoverished would our lives be if all that had survived of Chaplin's silent period were an early Keystone or two, and "The Kid." And in a very general sense, this is how we must regard the failure to preserve the output of W. C. Fields.

Why has this been allowed to happen? The answer quite simply is that Fields worked principally for Paramount, a good thing in that the company allowed him leeway to experiment with his as yet far from universally popular brand of comedy, but decidedly bad in another way. Always the most economy-minded of the major studios, Paramount spent as little as possible on the production of their movies, and nothing at all on their preservation. DeMille, when working for Paramount, had the funds and the facilities to undertake the preservation of his own films, and his estate now maintains a superb record of his work. Certain stars, such as Mary Pickford, also undertook the preservative work that should rightly have been done by the studio. Fields, lacking the funds or the technical production facilities to encompass such work, most likely never gave the matter a second thought. The result: through the years, the highly combustible old nitrate prints have been slowly decomposing in the vaults, and instead of being copied immediately when the danger signs appeared, the prints were junked. Even today, when television use of old footage and theatrical compilations have proved that the silent films have current commercial value, the process of destruction continues at this studio. Were it not for the film archives in many countries, many of the genuine masterpieces produced by Paramount in the teens and twenties would long since have been permanently lost, and indeed it is on such archives—The Museum of Modern Art in New York, the George Eastman House in Rochester, New York, the British Film Institute in London, the *Cinémathèque Française* in Paris, and a handful of others—that any future "history" of Paramount will depend. Fortunately, if belatedly, Metro-Goldwyn-Mayer and other studios have recognized the value of the film in their vaults, and have instituted preservation programs. Even if this decision is motivated by commercial reasons rather than by the wish to maintain a cultural heritage, it is a welcome one.

Admittedly, the great bulk of Fields' missing films were well covered by reviewers, coming as they did in the mid-twenties, heyday of film trade publications and fan magazines. It is easy enough to determine their story-lines and gags. But reviews of comedy in the twenties tended to ignore style, invention and, indeed, anything other than pure content. Both Keaton and Fields eschewed sentiment and out-and-out slapstick; their work, though vastly different, often involved elements of dry wit and especially black humor that was neither fully understood nor appreciated then. (Accordingly, early Keaton and Fields comedies seem far fresher today than those of Chaplin or Lloyd, cast in a more acceptable contemporary mold.) Too, the twenties were so rich in visual comedy that it was very quickly and easily taken for granted; critics tended to slight the familiar—even when good —in favor of the new and different. Thus Ernst Lubitsch's tasteful but rather static adaptation of Oscar Wilde's "Lady Windermere's Fan" was applauded for its wit and for breaking away from contemporary movie tradition, even though it was little more than a photographed play and largely devoid of the visual charm and imagination so prevalent in current Keaton and Lloyd films which were beginning to be dismissed as merely "more of the same." A good many critics of the twenties, Mordaunt Hall of *The New York Times* among them, seem to have been biased in favor of those Fields films that were based on plays as opposed to those created expressly for the screen by those concerned "only" with making movies. The "only" is Mr. Hall's adjective, and it is expressive of a surprisingly prevalent attitude of condescension to the movies in the twenties. Tastes in comedy vary far more from decade to decade than do tastes in drama, so the praises and the pans directed at the Fields movies in those years can be taken only as the roughest kind of guide to their real merits.

Are we then to approach Fields' career with defeatist forebodings that an accurate appraisal is impossible? Surprisingly, this is not the case. Frustrating though that huge gap is to both dyed-in-the-wool historians and Fields fanciers, it does not withhold vital information from us. Unlike Chaplin, and to a lesser extent Keaton and Langdon, Fields' screen character did not evolve gradually, nor did it pass from one clearly differentiated stage to another. In his first film, "Pool Sharks," a short, and more demonstrably in his first starring vehicle, 1925's "Sally of the Sawdust,"* the basic Fields screen character was already fully formed. What followed was not so much change as it was polishing in the best old vaudevillian tradition, the discarding of gags and bits of characterization that didn't work, and the retention and extension of those that did. This occurred in the roughly parallel development of the comedy of Laurel and Hardy. While some of their finest shorts were silent, one could form an accurate estimate of their methods and creative abilities from their sound output and one or two examples of their silent films. Their basic screen characters never changed, and neither did their methods of construction and per-

* Based on Fields' 1923 Broadway success, "Poppy."

formance. Individual gags that they liked they repeated regularly; complete sequences that worked well were frequently duplicated intact, or with minor variations, in subsequent films; and whole plot-lines sometimes were reused three or four times in films that never were regarded as "official" re-makes.

This applies equally to Fields. And when sound came in, Laurel and Hardy as well as Fields found themselves with voices that suited their screen images perfectly, and they had the imagination to use sound effects and music with creative exaggeration so that their own unique little world, even in the more realistic milieu of the sound film, remained intact. Fields' nasal bray and the thrown-away insult were such an essential part of his makeup that it seems an unlikely claim that his silent comedy roles were complete without them; yet on the strength of his performance in "Sally of the Sawdust" one may justifiably state that this was so. Keaton and Langdon needed silence just as the Marx Brothers and Mae West had to have sound; Fields depended on neither, but like John Barrymore (a fine stage actor to whom the denial of speech never seemed a serious handicap) he was able to grab at sound and exploit it to the hilt. Because so many of Fields' sound features were re-workings or actual re-makes of his silents, and thus reflected that now-lost art of the vaudevillian's polishing of an act until it achieved perfection, it is not unreasonable to assume that his best talkies represent the best of his overall work. Viewed in this light, the vast concentration of vanished work from the twenties seems less serious in a purely historic context, though no less frustrating in terms of the hours of presumably fascinating entertainment now denied us.

W. C. Fields in his first motion picture, "Pool Sharks" (1915).

The first screen closeup of W. C. Fields; "Pool Sharks."

3

The First Film

"Pool Sharks" was Fields' first venture into motion pictures. It is perhaps less surprising that it should contain so much traditional Fieldsian fooling than that it is such a good short comedy by any standards.

By 1915 the movies were well out of their infancy; it was the year of D. W. Griffith's "The Birth of a Nation," and such directors as Herbert Brenon, Cecil B. DeMille and Maurice Tourneur already were making films of taste, subtlety and artistic merit. But comedy had been slow to develop and was still in its early stages, with slapstick of a not-too-inventive kind still outweighing all other types. Mack Sennett's sub-directors had not yet had time to gain expertise in the different approaches to sight comedy; Fatty Arbuckle and his comrades were still relying heavily on the pratfall, and only Chaplin, having moved from Sennett's Keystone to the Essanay Studios, could claim to have advanced the art of comedy to any marked degree.

Fields, then in his mid-thirties, was added to the growing ranks of screen comedians because of the need for new faces, and because the movies, always desperately trying to gain respectability and prestige, continually pillaged the stage for such big names as could be persuaded to condescend to the making of movies.

Apart from the instant success of Douglas Fairbanks, few stage players of the time really caught on in the movies, although many one- and two-reelers unknowingly performed a valuable service to show business history in recording for posterity some of the most popular vaudeville routines of the day. The subtle pantomime of Negro comic Bert Williams, a Ziegfeld top-liner, showed to advantage on the screen in such Biograph shorts as "A Natural Born Gambler" and "Fish." Fields, by now a vaudeville headliner as well as a Ziegfeld star, and apparently as big a name as he could ever hope to be, was signed by Gaumont Company for two films, one of which was to repeat his famous pool-game routine for which he was presumably very well paid. However, since there was no follow-up, one must assume that neither the public nor exhibitors were wildly enthusiastic. Quite probably Fields' very orderliness and restraint in the first short, "Pool Sharks," worked against it. Certainly the garden party and pool-room locales left the way wide open for the violent slapstick exchanges to which Mack Sennett had conditioned movie audiences, and yet Fields resolutely bypassed such opportunities. Slapstick and violence he used, but of the controlled, steadily building variety that was to mark not only Fields' later work but also that of Laurel and Hardy. Too, Fields offered an entirely new kind of comic lead who was neither hero nor heavy, physically almost repellent with his obnoxious little clip-on moustache, half-way between the aggressive but increasingly sympathetic comic hero of Chaplin and the gesticulating, anti-social comic villain of Ford Sterling.

"Pool Sharks" runs for a full, tightly packed reel, or approximately fifteen minutes at the rate of silent projection. It is a Fields vehicle from first to last, though curiously, in view of his stage popularity, there was no attempt to exploit Fields in any of the ways peculiar to the film medium. His entrance is casual, without build-up or special introduction, and his comedy and the action of the film are both well under way before we are given a single closeup of his face, although there have been other closeups. Telling its tale almost entirely visually, with few subtitles, "Pool Sharks" has little real story. The rivalry of Fields and his opponent for the hand of the heroine is the only plot-line, and the film is divided into two halves: garden-party by-play followed by the long pool-table sequence, with a quick and traditional knockabout climax.

Fields' first appearance could hardly be more typical. He saunters into a sunny garden, jauntily swinging a cane which promptly connects with his own head, a piece of business which, with such variations as trying to put a hat on his head and intercepting it with his cane, was to reappear in most of his later films. A well-paced series of pantomimic misfortunes allows him to sit on a pin, which he extracts in closeup and holds out for audience scrutiny; the pin out of the way, he sits down again, this time on a plate of marshmallows, and finally seeks the safety of a hammock, which collapses under him. Invited to join the other guests at the outdoor tea-table, he picks his chair and prepares, with great care, to lower himself into it. But his rival gets there first, and Fields finds himself almost sitting in the other man's lap. However, a hapless little boy already has a seat, and Fields neatly top-

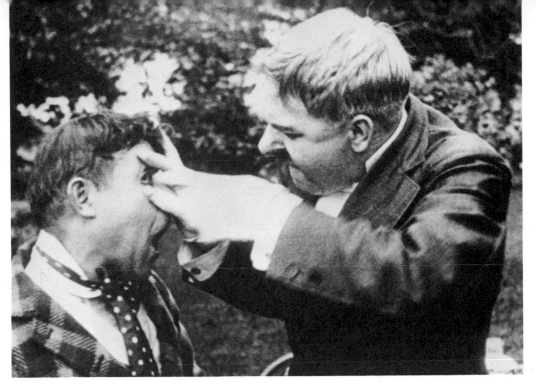

Fields crushes opposition; "Pool Sharks."

Fields, the sportsmanlike winner; "Pool Sharks."

ples him from it with a deft yank on his cane and appropriates his chair. Thus far, and in some initial comic byplay with the food, the action has been casual and almost underplayed, and since Fields has not yet been favored with a closeup, he has been presented as little more than a party-pest. Now, however—and quite logically, considering the action involved—the camera moves in for a closeup and we get our first really good look at Fields as he does battle with a stubborn stalk of asparagus which obstinately refuses to enter his open and receptive mouth and insists on poking him in the eye instead. Leaving Fields' inanimate enemies for a moment, the film establishes the rival's interest in the heroine. Gradually the pace begins to quicken: Fields is harassed by a pea-shooting brat of a boy, so much so at one point that Fields drops steaming coffee on the girl. The rival, aroused to fighting action by now, grabs Fields' nose and tweaks it, deliberately and painfully. Proud of his aggression, for he is a much shorter and frailer man than Fields, the rival stands back to survey the damage he has done, but, observing the signs of impending retaliation, he quickly covers his face with his hands. Not to be thwarted in his revenge, Fields laboriously pries open his tormentor's fingers, and through this chink in the armor ferociously pokes him in the eye. Now it is Fields' turn to stand back, and he seeks to end the brawl while he is the victor. He waves an admonishing finger at his foe, only to have it vigorously bitten. The heroine, it might be added, is supremely unconcerned at all the carnage wrought for her favors, and if she cares for either of the two men, the odds seem to be slightly in favor of Fields' diminutive opponent, an even less inspiring example of manhood than Fields.

The rivals now repair to the pool room to settle their differences through skill rather than brute strength. Again Fields comes up against the terrible machinations of the inanimate—in this case a piece of chalk, dangling from a string, that successfully eludes his attempts to grab it. The game is on. Fields' first shot splits the triangle of billiard balls, which form themselves into a regimented straight line and then resume their original triangle. His opponent's first shot achieves exactly the same result. Despite Fields' considerable skill with billiard balls, and a specially constructed table that "guided" the balls, this sequence enlarges on the original vaudeville skit, and brings into play limited trick stop-motion photography for some of the gag effects, though they are executed so smoothly that only the patent impossibility of the billiard-ball manipulations indicates their usage.

The order which seems to have been restored is, however, short-lived. With grandiose gestures, Fields twirls his cue, hits an innocent spectator in the eye, and follows through with a jab to the stomach. A misjudged shot lands a ball into another spectator's eye, and with elegant aplomb Fields keeps the game going by retrieving the ball from the man's face with his cue! Clearly the winner now, Fields plays with even greater fervor and self-confidence, and when a lineup of balls falls from the wall-racks onto the pool table, he calmly shoots them right back. His rival, an unsportsmanlike loser, takes his defeat hard and hits Fields a resounding crack

Fields, a moment of triumph; "Pool Sharks."

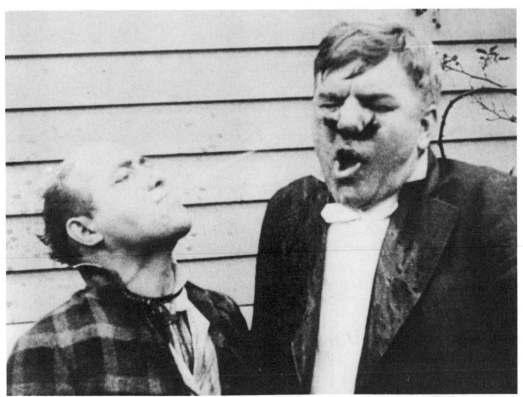

Fields: victory can be painful when it is standing on your foot; "Pool Sharks."

on the head with his cue. At this Fields quickly works himself into an uncontrollable temper and starts to hurl billiard balls in all directions. One careens through a window, breaks a hanging fish bowl and drenches the heroine, who, with live fish flopping in her hair, finally loses her apathy toward the conduct of the two rivals.

As the ball-throwing orgy continues, Fields gets soundly clobbered, while one of his missiles whisks away a spectator's toupee. The heroine expresses her extreme annoyance. The rival leaps head first through a window to land in a rain barrel. Fields rushes through a trapdoor into the cellar, which fortuitously is well stocked with liquor. Grabbing the handiest bottle, he makes his escape as all the other guests tumble down the stairs. In the garden again, Fields has a momentary flash of compassion and gallantry and pauses to rescue his head-down drowning rival from the rain barrel. However, the ungrateful wretch shows his appreciation by squirting a stream of water into Fields' face. Incensed, but with his rage now under control, Fields carefully replaces the ingrate in the rain barrel and ambles off to enjoy his stolen liquor.

Knowing Fields as we do today, it is fascinating to see so many of his routines and mannerisms at their filmic beginning, and we find ourselves supplying the oaths, curses and snide insults that we know Fields would have employed had the film been a talkie. Nevertheless, considerations of nostalgia and hindsight apart, "Pool Sharks" must surely rank as one of the most auspicious debuts made by any of the major screen comedians. Certainly it took Chaplin, to cite the most obvious example, a long period of trial, error and experiment to reach the stage that Fields has here achieved so effortlessly in his very first film. And while there may have been funnier comedies prior to "Pool Sharks," there were surely none so well controlled, so mathematically precise in their timing, or so selective in their use of slapstick. Largely forgotten, and certainly unseen for many years (a single thirty-five-millimeter print was rediscovered only in the mid 1960's), "Pool Sharks" is a minor masterpiece when viewed in the context of its period, and certainly a major milestone in the early evolution of screen comedy.

In view of the merits of "Pool Sharks," one can only conjecture as to whether Fields' second short for Gaumont surpassed or even maintained its quality. Obviously, there was no time for Fields to have studied movie technique and applied the lessons of the first to the production of the second. Both films were shot almost at the same time in Flushing, while Fields was performing in the Ziegfeld Follies in New York. Much publicity was given to Ziegfeld's gracious waiving of contractual exclusivity in order to let Fields make his film debut. "Pool Sharks," directed by the now forgotten Edwin Middleton, went into release in September, and the second Fields comedy one-reeler (made by William Haddock, an Edison director) followed in October. Entitled "His Lordship's Dilemma," it presented Fields as a remittance man with Bud Ross as his valet. All that remains of this film are the tantalizing but rather uninformative ads placed in the trade papers by the Mutual Company (distributors of the film) showing Fields swinging a golf club!

W. C. Fields as Eustace McGargle in "Sally of the Sawdust"; 1925.

4.

Hearst, Griffith and Eustace McGargle

For almost a decade after making "Pool Sharks" and "His Lordship's Dilemma," Fields worked exclusively on the stage. In successive editions of "The Ziegfeld Follies" and "George White's Scandals," he entrenched himself as one of the foremost comedians and certainly the most entertaining juggler of the day. His popularity and his salary checks grew steadily, but this plateau, while increasingly profitable, seemed to hold little creative future. Then, unexpectedly, the movies beckoned again, and Fields signed for a role in one of the Hearst-Cosmopolitan vehicles for Marion Davies, a Revolutionary War story, "Janice Meredith."

No complete prints of this film are known to have survived, so appraisal of Fields' importance to it, or the skill he showed, is difficult. Like most of the Marion Davies vehicles, it was visually a very handsome production, and it was an expensive one. Also, in keeping with the Hearst policy of spotlighting the star as much as possible, the hero was played by Harrison Ford, whose slight build and somewhat effeminate manner hardly qualified him for the role of the passionate lover and gallant patriot, Charles Fownes. As a film of major importance, "Janice Meredith" would seem to have been doomed from the start. Its elaborate plottings made it seem trivial, especially since D. W. Griffith's superb epic of the Revolutionary War, "America," was being made almost simultaneously, offering stunning near-documentary reconstructions of major battles and events as well as all the showmanship of romance and last-minute rescues. Aware of the shortcomings in his own film, Hearst approached Griffith and asked him not to include the famous episode of Washington crossing the Delaware, so that it could be used as the big highlight sequence of the Davies film. Griffith acquiesced graciously, and in return the Hearst papers extravagantly promoted and endorsed "America" when it was released. Curiously, this is one of the episodes from "Janice Meredith" that has survived; though little more than an elaborate copy of traditional heroic paintings of the event, still it is a stirring and visually exciting sequence. Neither Miss Davies nor Fields appears in the episode.

Everybody in the cast but Fields is clearly identified by a character name, from George Washington to Lords Howe and Cornwallis. The name-dropping even extended beyond the official cast, for Ken Maynard, soon to become a major western star, made his unbilled debut in this film as Paul Revere. Yet Fields was a little more than half-way down the cast sheet, identified only as "A British Sergeant." Clearly he was there in what amounted to a guest-star vignette, although this was well before the days when such practices became common; equally clearly his presence was beneficial to the film. Even if only in passing, most of the reviewers referred to Fields' comedy scenes as the drunken soldier. Fields had the happy knack of looking perfectly at home in period costume or uniform, and he seemed well suited in his red coat and three-cornered hat. Admittedly, his somewhat disarrayed powdered wig and his insistence on retaining his usual moustache did work against an image of complete conviction.

By one of those felicitous coincidences where the right man is in the right place at the right time—combinations of circumstances that also made stars of Rudolph Valentino and Clark Gable—Fields was trying to break the deadlock clamped on him by vaudeville just at the time when a new musical comedy, "Poppy," by Dorothy Donnelly, was being readied for Broadway. Fields knew nothing of the play, but its producer knew of Fields and of the carefully leaked information that Fields wanted to branch out.

The key role in "Poppy" is that of one Eustace McGargle, a cunning modern charlatan with an inflated ego, devoted to the theory that only suckers work, and prepared to devote all of his energies and waking hours to fleecing them—most notably in the appropriate atmosphere of small county fairs. Although Fields had always been too afraid of losing to enter the sporting arena of the con-men and card-sharks, he had loved to pose as the slicker who could outsmart all comers, while his harsh yet ingratiating voice and his exuberant magnification of the English language further established his kinship with Miss Donnelly's fictional character. McGargle had not been written with Fields in mind, but he well could have been, just as Sydney Greenstreet has always seemed the model for Dashiell Hammett's Gutman in "The Maltese Falcon," even though the picture was made more than a decade after the novel's appearance.

Despite a slight reduction in the salary he had been getting as a vaudeville headliner, Fields signed for "Poppy" and took over the role of Eustace McGargle. From then on, every role he played was to be a repetition or slight variation of this character, with such personal embellishments as child-baiting and displays of virtuoso juggling even though Miss Donnelly had somehow not had the foresight to include such antics in her initial manuscript. Many of these Fieldsian traits he injected into McGargle from the very beginning, changing and refining the character throughout rehearsals, so that when McGargle finally bowed on the New York stage at the Apollo Theatre on September third, 1923, the character owed almost as much to Fields as to its creator. The show was an instant success. Although there were those critics who found the story old-fashioned and the music undistinguished, the majority were pleased and all agreed in acclaiming Fields as a major comic talent. That many of his routines were familiar mattered as little then as it would subsequently in his movies, and the transformation of a skilled vaudeville performer into a comedy actor capable of creating a fully rounded portrait of a larcenous yet lovable rascal was one of the theatrical highlights of the year.

Fields played in "Poppy" for over a year, and inevitably it was bought for the movies. Happily—though not so inevitably—Fields was also signed to star in the film. In his biography, Robert Lewis Taylor devotes nearly two pages to this film, not only as Fields' first major film work, but as the occasion for his first head-on collision with studio policies. It should be remembered that in 1949, when Taylor's book was published, the film version of "Poppy," which was to be retitled "Sally of the Sawdust," had been unseen for nearly twenty years and was presumed lost. Reappraisal of the film at that time was impossible. Further, in 1949, while such items as baseball scores were considered of paramount importance, and the inaccurate reporting of a ball game of two decades earlier prompted columns of outraged corrections in the offending newspaper, film history was considered so esoteric (and insignificant) a field that even well-informed writers seldom troubled to be factual. Even today, there is far too little regard for accuracy in the field of film history, but from the mid-50's on, so much has been written on the movies' past that there is no longer any excuse for the unchecked fact. In 1949 the situation was so different that Taylor states sweepingly that Paramount deliberately whittled away at Fields' role in "Sally of the Sawdust" in order to build the film into a Carol Dempster starring vehicle, although Paramount did not produce the picture, and none of Miss Dempster's movies were ever really "vehicles" for her. Certainly the most was not made of Fields, but then what screen comedian ever was used to his best potential so early in his career?

"Sally of the Sawdust" was produced by David Wark Griffith for his own company and for release through United Artists. Griffith had many reasons for being cautious. His personal fortunes had been declining of late. A film-maker of integrity, he had refused to turn out the slick jazz-age comedies and sex dramas so much in vogue at the box office then, but had continued to make films that he believed in and did best: the vivid spectacle of the French Revolution, "Orphans of the Storm," historical sagas such as the epic of American history called "America," and films with themes of social comment, as in the beautiful but unremittingly grim "Isn't Life Wonderful?" which concerned inflation and hunger in post-war Germany.

Admittedly past his creative prime, he was by no means as outdated as his critics claimed, and his decline was notable only in a commercial sense. When he made "Sally of the Sawdust," it was clear that his days of total independence were over. He was already in the process of closing his large studio in Mamaroneck, New York, and had been signed to a contract by Paramount Pictures. Anxious to have him start work for them, Paramount even made their Long Island studios available to him for much of "Sally of the Sawdust," so that Griffith could be free with the minimum of delay.

Griffith was much in need of a good commercial property, and "Sally of the Sawdust" seemed to fit the bill. Despite Fields' huge success on the Broadway stage, he was still not a movie name, and it is understandable that Griffith might be unwilling to gamble on Fields in the most important role. That Fields was even hired for the picture is an astonishing tribute to his impact in the role, for Hollywood to this day has still to be convinced of the value of signing Broadway actors for film versions of their stage hits, as witness the refusal to entrust "My Fair Lady" to Julie Andrews.

It is also extraordinary that Fields was signed, because Griffith was never very sure of himself with comedy. In a purely dramatic sense, he knew just when to punctuate his films with a moment of light relief, when to interpolate a comedy bit so that suspense could be brought to a climax, relaxed, and then built again. But sustained comedy in his hands usually seemed forced; the comedy of Creighton Hale, for instance, in "Way Down East" and "Orphans of the Storm," had been the only weak elements of those films. Fortunately, the silent cinema removed the elements of music and comedy patter from "Sally of the Sawdust," and what remained was a plot-line containing many of the elements of Dickensian coincidence and sentiment of which Griffith was a past master. With the elimination of the musical framework, the shifting of emphasis to this plot-line was certainly understandable. As to the suggestion that the film was deliberately turned from a Fields vehicle into a Dempster vehicle, it must be stressed that, with the possible exception of "Way Down East" which was tailored to Lillian Gish, none of Griffith's films could ever have been termed vehicles for their stars.

Plot and style always meant more to Griffith than a star, and most of his players, well aware of this, were quite willing to sacrifice billing prestige and pref-

McGargle (Fields) with his ward (Carol Dempster) in a heated moment; "Sally of the Sawdust."

erential treatment for the privilege of appearing in his films. In any case, Carol Dempster was never a sufficiently important player to warrant the film being drastically re-shaped in her favor. Griffith was reportedly very much in love with her and, it was said, had asked her to marry him, but even this personal involvement would never have caused him to place her above the film as a whole. A variable actress, brilliant in "Isn't Life Wonderful?," in other films too often she gave performances that were clearly imitative of Lillian Gish and Mae Marsh. She was certainly never a "star" in the accepted sense of the word; she made only a couple of films away from Griffith, and would probably not have survived in movies as long as she did without his sponsorship.

There was friction between Griffith and Fields, and the film bears this out quite plainly. Fields, never one for discipline, must have been hard-pressed to understand Griffith's methods, while Griffith, unused to having his autocratic rule questioned, can only have found Fields' free-wheeling independence and bizarre sense of humor intolerable. The film almost suggests that the two units went their separate ways, Fields doing pretty much as he liked and coming up with a forerunner of "You Can't Cheat an Honest Man," and Griffith concentrating on pastoral New England and the romantic aspects of the story to produce a light variation on "Way Down East." Several quick shots of juggling routines suggest further that Griffith was tactful enough to appear to give in, and to shoot scenes in the way Fields demanded, in the safe knowledge that apart from their use as establishing shots or cutaways, such scenes could be edited out later.

It is the editing, rather than any attempts to build up the heroine's role, that hampers Fields' effect more than anything else. His best comedy sequences in "Sally of the Sawdust" are like vaudeville routines, and once begun need to be left severely alone so that they can build to their climax without interference. But too often Griffith cut away from Fields in the middle of a routine, not to minimize his work, but because it was Griffith's cutting method to interweave themes and characters, and to develop story threads in parallel action so that their ultimate joining near the end of the film would provide a climax of double unity. Such methods had worked magnificently in "The Birth of a Nation" and in "Orphans of the Storm," but Griffith failed to see that meticulously constructed comedy could not be interrupted as could drama. Moreover, apart from this preconceived structure imposed by Griffith's methods, the film was apparently reworked substantially after completion, in order to heighten the suspense of a typical Griffith chase ending.

Elements of time and geography are all awry in this climactic chase. Fields, captured by bootleggers, escapes and rushes to the aid of the heroine, who in her turn has broken out of the courtroom where she was being tried, and is now being pursued by police. It is obvious that the juxtaposition of the two escapes and two pursuits was not planned quite as it emerged, and that logic and time lapses were brushed aside for the sake of injecting as much chase and tension as possible into the final reel. One might also add that, while Griffith had been growing a little careless in his editing for some time past, none of his films had ever been edited as badly as this one. Much of the cutting was slipshod in the extreme, lacking many of the barest elementaries of continuity. Cuts from medium shots to close-ups would show the players in non-matching positions, and sometimes even the backgrounds did not match. Much of this carelessness undoubtedly can be attributed to the haste with which Griffith finished and assembled the film in order to be free to start his Paramount commitments. However, in fairness to both Griffith and Fields, while the editing seems unforgivable when one studies the film alone, if public showings before highly responsive New York audiences in the early 1960's are a criterion, both Griffith's pacing and Fields' comedy seemed to work perfectly.

Filming in the East, Griffith obtained most of his supporting players from the New York stage, though, surprisingly, not from the company of "Poppy." For his key supporting roles, Griffith selected Erville Alderson (whom he had used twice before), Effie Shannon, Glenn Anders (effective in some lecherous villainy a full twenty years before he became well known in films for his portrayal of a vicious sadist in Orson Welles' "The Lady from Shanghai") and, as the hero, Alfred Lunt. About the most passive of all the Griffith heroes, the character as played by Lunt enjoyed some charming rural love scenes with Carol Dempster, was absent when she needed him most (an unlikely plot device sending him out of town as her tribulations began) and returned just in time to rescue her from the McGargle environment and elevate her to his high social standing through marriage.

The plot of "Sally of the Sawdust" gets under way with those elements so beloved by Griffith: a prologue separating mother from daughter, and the establishing of social barriers which true love ultimately will overcome. Against the wishes of his gentle wife, tyrannical old Judge Foster throws his daughter out into the world because she has dared to marry a circus performer. Conveniently, and for medical or other reasons not stated, both young husband and young wife soon die, and on her death-bed the wife leaves her little girl to the care of Eustace McGargle, side-show faker.

Fields, gaudily attired in checkered pants, his lip adorned by his traditional and most unappealing clip-on moustache, rapidly establishes that he will display none of the sentiment lavished by Chaplin on Jackie Coogan in "The Kid," and makes it equally plain that he's going to inject his own favorite little pieces of business as early and as frequently as possible. Writing a letter, he has the ink-bottle adjacent to a cup of tea, and of course dips the nib into the tea. Before long we are treated to the inevitable loss of his hat, which gets detoured on to his upraised stick.

Years pass, and Sally grows up under McGargle's tutelage, dancing and performing trapeze acrobatics as a crowd-gathering warm-up to her foster-father's juggling act. In this initial carnival sequence at least, Fields has the benefit of sustained closeups as he juggles deftly, bringing in his old vaudeville gimmick of pretending to drop a ball and then cunningly retrieving it by bouncing it back into orbit with his elbow. One can sense Fields' pleasure in this scene from the almost diabolical grin on his face, a grin which bespeaks not only genuine pride in his skill, but satisfaction at having got the scene into the picture.

Juggling is but a part of the McGargle repertoire, and most of the easy money is to be made behind the tent by means of the old shell game—despite his many promises to Sally to give it up. McGargle is not averse to a little pocket-picking, though here his skill is matched by that of the circus elephant who sidles up behind McGargle, waits for him to steal a wallet, and then purloins it from McGargle's pocket with his trunk. Sally's involvement in a "Hey Rube!" fight in which she loyally fights by McGargle's side, and an attempt by circus trapeze star Glenn Anders to rape her, convince McGargle that it is time to take her away from the circus environment.

He is offered a carnival job in a town called Green Meadows, and since that is where her grandparents (now very wealthy) live, he decides to attempt a reunion. The journey to Green Meadows on limited funds is fraught with minor perils. Sally spends their last quarter with a railway station vendor to buy a hot dog and the cigar so essential to the McGargle appearance of affluence. They wind up riding hunched together on the steps outside the railway car, where the animosity of a group of railroad bums, along with a torrential downpour, causes them to be dumped, bruised and soaked, from the train.

Fortunately they are deposited in Green Meadows, but before they can seek the carnival, some semblance of sartorial elegance has to be restored. Together they wander through the town and find a baker hard at work. He offers to let them warm up and dry their clothes if they'll tend his kilns while he is away. Sally dutifully goes to work, but McGargle climbs into a warm kiln for a snooze. In a sequence combining slapstick with black humor that could have been hilarious without Griffith's cutaways to other action, but is still very funny, Sally energetically piles coal on the dormant fires, blissfully unaware that she is baking her foster-father along with the loaves. Inadvertently locked in his kiln, McGargle stirs uneasily as his nether regions begin to scorch and smoke, twists and turns in his sleep, and finally comes to with the horrified realization of his predicament. Unable to stand upright, he hops around on hands and knees on the increasingly hot kiln floor, until Sally, who has been searching for him, finally hears his cries and comes to release him. But when the oven door swings open, he is too overcome with heat to climb out, and collapses. Just as McGargle is about to be burned to a crisp, Sally picks up one of the huge wooden ladles used for placing the loaves in the kiln and, gingerly easing McGargle onto it, pulls him out to safety.

As he stands fanning the smoke away from his still smouldering trousers, he notices with some surprise that Sally has suddenly acquired a rather prominent bosom. Always aware of their precarious eating habits, she has provided for future emergencies by stuffing some of the bakery's buns into her dress. "My, you *are* growing up, Sally!" McGargle remarks, scratching his head, his face still a study in disbelief that such things can literally happen overnight.

The best piece of sustained comedy in the film, although performed without the standard Fields characteristics, this baking-kiln sequence plays extremely well today, and is both expertly timed and interestingly underplayed by Fields, although unfortunately the cumulative effect is lessened by Griffith's cutaway in the middle of the action to re-establish the character of Sally's grandfather.

At a charity bazaar McGargle's professional skill is applauded, but it is made abundantly clear that in this high-toned Connecticut community circus folk are still frowned on socially. Nonetheless, Sally meets and falls in love with Peyton Lennox (Alfred Lunt), socially prominent son of a close friend of her grandfather, Judge Foster. Their gentle and quite sensitive romantic scenes—which begin, with surprising effectiveness, in a cemetery—are charmingly done.

Partly for economy reasons and partly because the story logically permits it, a great deal of the film is shot out of doors. No other Griffith film—not even "Way Down East"—used outdoor locations so extensively. The lack of substance in the plot material prevents any dramatic or symbolic use of landscape, a favorite device of Griffith's in earlier days, but the very charm and beauty of so many of the exteriors is one of the film's major assets.

McGargle's initial attempts to introduce Sally to her rich relatives fail. A visit to the Foster mansion—their rise to unexplained affluence must have taken place at a dizzying rate—is sabotaged by McGargle's encounter with a playful little puppy. The estate's gardener has been watering the flower beds, and inadvertently has sprinkled the McGargle trousers. The puppy, an entirely innocent bystander, gazes in naïve friendliness as Fields discovers his dampened trouser-legs, jumps to the obvious conclusion, and kicks the offending canine out of the scene. His wrath now fully aroused, he is with difficulty dissuaded from heaving bricks at the stately house, and the family reunion is delayed until another occasion.

Sally gets her introduction to high society through Peyton Lennox, however, who engages her as a dancer at an elaborate party. Sally, stunningly gowned, is an instant hit and touches the heart of the judge's wife, who is still pining for her dead daughter and is of course unaware that this girl is her own granddaughter. Lennox's father, however, disapproves of his son's romantic inclinations, and in order to break up the match he sends Peyton out of town. Judge Foster's legal influence is sought in an effort either to run the McGargles out of town or to place them behind bars. The opportunity soon presents itself when McGargle is caught fleecing the suckers once again. Sally, entirely innocent of any involvement, lets herself be caught in order to give McGargle time to make his getaway.

While Sally awaits her fate in prison, McGargle, out in the Connecticut wilds, has fallen in with bootleggers. In a hazily written sequence they somehow recognize him for what he is, after having suspected him of being a revenue agent, but insist that he remain their prisoner until the morning. This rather labored device is employed to add suspense and delays to the final situations. McGargle escapes, however, steals an old jalopy, and the bootleggers give chase. As in the baking-kiln episode, the effect of this lively episode is lessened by Griffith's constant cross-cutting to Carol Dempster's trial, which is conducted with all the heavy seriousness of the murder trial in "Intolerance," and not always helped by the florid titling. "If only he knew he was torturing his baby's baby!" is one subtitle given to the stern and merciless judge!

The chase sequences, though they have no real time to build, do contain some memorable Fieldsian images: McGargle coaxing his slow-to-start auto up a hill by pushing at the road with a thin twig, or later, roaring and bouncing across an open field, slapping the side of his jalopy with a switch, like a jockey urging his mount to greater endeavors.

Another delightful bit of business, surely of Fields' own conception, is a run-in with a policeman, the first of many such Fieldsian encounters. The auto has a low top; as Fields takes his leave of the officer of the law, he tips his hat, and since he can't get it back on his head, the hat winds up on the roof of the car, directly *over* his head. This is a matter of but temporary concern, for Fields' none-too-gentle handling of the jalopy eventually results in bouncing his head through the roof to the waiting hat. Moments later the whole roof is ripped off anyway. Sally in the meantime has made her escape from the courtroom by leaping from a window, climbing down a tree, and leading the police a merry chase with some typical Fairbanks acrobatics.

The rather erratic editing of these intercut sequences is emphasized by the obvious fact that some of the Fields scenes were clearly intended originally for different time periods, and the different threads of action are drawn together rather clumsily. The bootleggers, having served their sole function of providing delaying tactics, are dropped arbitrarily. The roughness of some of the cutting is further evidenced when an obvious double is used for Fields in some of the trickier stunt scenes, and the chase comes to an unexpectedly abrupt end when the jalopy crashes and Fields' double suffers a nasty fall. This seems to have fazed Griffith not at all; he merely inserts a closeup of Fields looking dazed and falling back unconscious, paving the way for his ultimate arrival in the courtroom, ruffled but uninjured, just in time to save the recaptured Sally from being sentenced, and to reveal that she is the judge's granddaughter. The case is promptly dropped, a hardly salutary comment on nepotism in Connecticut justice, and Sally is restored both to grandparents and to a fortuitously returning hero.

In a climax visually reminiscent of Chaplin, Fields, presumably ennobled by this act of self-sacrifice, walks off alone, in long shot, down a little country lane. But before the sentimental iris-out can bring the adventure to this Chaplinesque finish, Fields is reclaimed by the now loving Foster family, who insist that he remain with them. Their unfortunate mistake is all too apparent in the closing scene as McGargle, dressed with a new elegance and having attached himself like a leech to their social prominence, takes them on a tour of his new property in his slick new automobile. McGargle has gone into the real estate business, and has raised the shell game to a level where his suckers can be fleeced of thousands rather than pennies!

Throughout "Sally of the Sawdust" there was never any question that it was Fields' film all the way—and despite the loving, caressing attention paid to Carol Dempster via the camerawork of Harry Fischbeck. All the basics of the Fields screen image are present, plus a generous supply of his favorite sight gags. The lack of any really funny lines of dialogue, even in title form, indicates, however, that it wasn't *what* Fields said that was usually funny, but the tones of exasperation, frustration, long-suffering patience and sarcasm with which he could turn the most commonplace of lines into gems of wit. So engaging was his personality, and so adroit his bits of visual "business," that no one felt cheated at being deprived of his voice. Critics generally liked the film, even though it was then fashionable to rap Griffith for his old-time sentiment and the lack of dynamism in his current films. Most critics conceded that his concessions to popular appeal with this particular property were justified. There was *no* divergence of opinion on W. C. Fields. The consensus was that a major new comedian had arrived on the screen.

Fields as Elmer Prettywilly in his first starring vehicle, "It's the Old Army Game." (Courtesy of Paramount Pictures)

☞ **5.**

The Long Island Years

Fields spent the three years from 1926 at Paramount's Long Island studio, turning out no fewer than eight starring vehicles. This was a lot of concentrated exposure for one comic, especially at a time when the established comedians were making one or at most two features a year. The Fields films were surprisingly short, however, often running just a few minutes under or over an hour. This length is undoubtedly as much as they could sustain, yet such brief footage posed a marketing problem in those days before the widespread growth of the double-bill system. Of those eight features, not one is known to have survived.

At this period there was such a rich lineup of comedy talent on the screen that it would seem there was neither room nor need for any new faces. As it was, some of the well-established comedians (the debonair and underrated Charlie Chase, for example) never reached their full potential, simply because of a glut on the comedy market and because they weren't sufficiently unique to be set apart from the rest. Yet Harry Langdon, last of the really great silent pantomimic clowns, was only just coming into his own; Laurel and Hardy were still working separately and would not team until 1926; and Will Rogers seemed already to be finished as a screen comedian. That left Fields, whose film career proper was launched at roughly the same time as Harry Langdon's—and seemed doomed to be much shorter.

Ironically, Langdon ultimately failed because of the border-line quality of his comedy. It could easily change from sensitive innocence to tasteless senility. Langdon needed a firm controlling hand. Under Frank Capra, Langdon had that control. But after three comedy masterpieces, Langdon decided that he could write and direct his own material, and he quickly lost contact with his own special reality and with his audience. Not only did he become less funny, he became almost incomprehensible. His decline was sudden and rapid.

Fields, on the other hand, had had no such impetus with which to launch his film career—certainly nothing like three masterpieces in a row to establish his claim to celluloid greatness. But despite the weaknesses of many of his early films, his character somehow struck a sympathetic spark. During the prohibition years of the twenties, when most of the virtues were considered old hat and when everyone who took a drink was automatically a law-breaker, audiences could readily sympathize with a character who chiseled and connived and to whom an uninterrupted supply of liquor was an essential way of life. Chaplin was a sentimental nobleman, Lloyd a go-getting young fellow who wouldn't take a drink even if it was legal, and Keaton a somnambulist who never really seemed part of this world, let alone of the period and geography of the American twenties. Fields was the only major comedian with a larcenous heart and wayward feet set firmly on contemporary Yankee soil, and that fact came to his rescue when disappointing early films might well have nipped his career in the bud.

Working at the Long Island studios had both advantages and drawbacks. The chief advantage lay in having William Le Baron as a production head. An adroit businessman and producer, he was also an expert practitioner of the art of soothing ruffled artistic temperaments, and had the wit and foresight to permit players and directors a much freer hand than they would have enjoyed under the more rigid front office supervision at the West Coast studios. Players and other film-makers who worked under Le Baron recall him with genuine affection, not because he gave in to their salary and other demands (often he couldn't and didn't), but because he treated them as individuals and artists rather than as mere contractual property.

The disadvantages of working in Long Island were purely mechanical ones. The studio was modern and expertly equipped and had one huge stage. It was ideal for such costume romances and dramas as "Dr. Jekyll and Mr. Hyde" and "Monsieur Beaucaire" that had to be played out against studio-created sets. But the surrounding environs of New York and New Jersey offered little variety in terms of outdoor locations, and unless the films in production there were specifically set in New York (such as "Love 'Em and Leave 'Em" and "Glorifying the American Girl," which made excellent use of Central Park locations) they tended to have a cramped look. Either New Jersey scenery had to double, rather drably and unconvincingly, for more colorful locales, or the "exteriors" were recreated in the studio.

This probably didn't hamper Fields personally; to him everything was but a backdrop for his comedy routines, and the blatant use of back projection in many of his later films confirmed that even a superficial realism was never one of his major concerns. But since his films invariably included many location sequences, those made solely in and around the Long Island studio probably suffered from the inevitable cramped "East Coast look." Of course, not all were rigidly limited to the studio, and where the plot elements were sufficiently important to justify the added expense, there were location jaunts to both Florida and California.

For his first Paramount film, it was logical that Fields should have been re-united with D. W. Griffith and Carol Dempster in an effort to repeat and expand the moderate commercial success of their "Sally of the Sawdust." Once again, Fields was the lovable scoundrel and Carol Dempster his daughter. The plot was a fairly routine piece of stock melodrama, with the heroine innocently involved in a murder investigation, and conveniently falling out of love with a weak-charactered musician (played by Harrison Ford) when she meets and falls in love instead with James Kirkwood, the crusading district attorney. (The ultra-moral and even puritanical District Attorney, best exemplified by Thomas Meighan in Cecil B. DeMille's 1923 "Manslaughter," became a fairly stock movie hero during the twenties when so many jazz-age heroines had to be shown the light and even to ex-piate their moral violations by sojourns in jail.

Neither Kirkwood nor Ford was a top name, and Fields was inserted into the film as a kind of insurance. But as a major character the girl's father had no valid place in the film, and there were universal complaints that Fields was shamefully wasted. Too, the trite story-line needed nowhere near the eleven reels that Griffith devoted to it, and in an effort to justify the film as a "prestige" item, Griffith re-verted to a typical chase, suspense and spectacle climax with an elaborately staged cyclone, which appears to have served its purpose in saving the entertainment day. While undoubtedly the film was a time-waster as far as Fields is concerned, it would be presumptuous to dismiss it as unworthy of Griffith purely on the grounds of the contemporary reviews.

Griffith's second Paramount film, "The Sorrows of Satan," was likewise dis-missed as sub-standard, and since the film was not seen for some thirty years, the glib criticism was repeated and unchallenged for all of that time. Seen today, "The Sorrows of Satan" is quite remarkable, and in many ways one of Griffith's most interesting works. On the basis of that film's evidence, Griffith would seem to have adjusted to his loss of independence rather quickly. He may no longer have had choice of subject or total autonomy of production control, but the efficiency and discipline of working in a major studio seem in many ways to have helped him. "The Sorrows of Satan" has superb lighting, camerawork and set design, and is one of the most handsome films Griffith ever produced. It is also one of the neatest, entirely devoid of the shipshod editing and production carelessness that marred "Sally of the Sawdust."

"That Royle Girl," which is one of the very few Griffith films to be totally missing today, may well have been a much better film than the reviewers of 1926 led us to believe. The real pity of it all is that Griffith, despite his lack of a cinematic sense of humor, and Fields, far from easy to place in the fairly limited gallery of Griffithian characters, were never able to find a common meeting ground from which a successful collaboration might have grown. That meeting ground might well have been Dickens, had not the twenties been the worst possible time for the American movie market to absorb such material.

Griffith himself adored Dickens' works, read them avidly, and considered their literary cross-cuttings and manipulations of plot coincidences the foundation of his own film style. Indeed, much of his earlier film work had consisted of literal reshapings of Dickens' stories into American surroundings. "True Heart Susie," one of Griffith's 1919 rural romances, is a fairly compact amalgam of "David Copperfield" and "Great Expectations," with many characters and situations transposed directly. Fields' preoccupation with Dickens, whom he read and re-read, was mainly with an intense study of the characters, whose picturesque traits often overlapped his own. Small wonder that he slipped into the shoes of Mr. Micawber so comfortably when he made "David Copperfield" in the thirties.

A wholehearted Dickensian collaboration between Griffith and Fields—"A Christmas Carol" perhaps, or "The Pickwick Papers"—would have been a joy to behold. But apart from some early Biograph one-reelers, Griffith never made an "official" Dickens adaptation, and, "David Copperfield" apart, none of the other movie versions of Dickens novels were to benefit from the marvelous physical and dramatic presence of Fields.

"It's the Old Army Game" was the second of the three films that Fields made in 1926, and his first starring vehicle. It introduced him to Edward Sutherland, a handsome director who had once been a leading man for Sennett and who hit it off with Fields right away. They became firm friends and continued to work together after the talkie era came in. Sutherland was never an inspired comedy director, but he was versatile (some of his best films were not comedies), skilled at setting up sight gags, and able to keep even slim material skipping along at a merry pace. "It's the Old Army Game," though not remembered with any great enthusiasm by Louise Brooks, the film's leading lady and both a friend and admirer of Fields, did get good reviews and garnered Fields his best movie notices to date.

The title seems to have been a pin-the-tail-on-the-donkey affair, for despite its suggestion of a continuation of McGargle's fleecing of suckers, the title had no real relation to the film's content. Basically the film was a rather shapeless collection of Fields' old stage skits, then new to most movie audiences, and all of them due to be repeated and improved upon in later Fields films. Fields is a small-

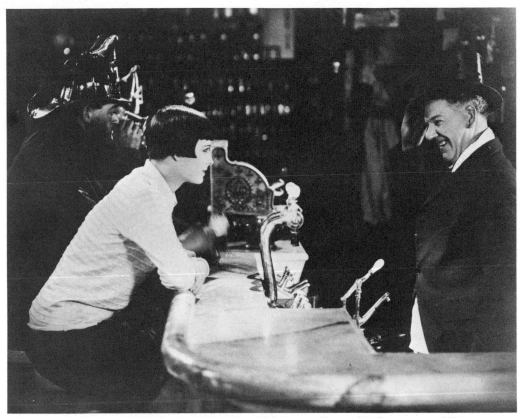

Fields, with Louise Brooks, in "It's the Old Army Game." (Courtesy of Paramount
Pictures)

town druggist, and the opening sequence finds him wakened in the middle of the
night by a woman who wishes to buy a two-cent stamp, a routine exploited at
much greater length in a short "The Pharmacist" which he made later, with
sound. His subsequent attempts to get back to sleep are thwarted by a noisy garbage collector, the clanging and shunting of an early morning train, and other
disturbances.

Fragments of this sequence have survived, and they indicate that it was fairly
carefully built but considerably less successful than its repetition in the talkie,
"It's a Gift." For full effect, this sequence depends on the skilled manipulation
of exaggerated sound effects, the deliberate rhythm of certain noises, and the
withholding of sound at times. In "It's a Gift," the same sequence runs for over
a reel, and is one of the funniest sequences ever put on film, by Fields or by anyone
else.

What is left of his silent version of the routine is a valuable indication of
the probable shortcomings of many of his earlier films. While his character could
be very funny without dialogue, the old stage routines, even though they were still

essentially visual, did need the punctuation of sound. Fields' attempt to sleep on the creaky porch chair just doesn't work without the sound of the unoiled squeaks and creaks, despite attempts to make it visual by closeups of straining springs. The climax of the film is a picnic on a private estate that Fields erroneously believes is for sale, and which is turned into a welter of litter and garbage. While this may well have worked better on a visual level than the earlier one, some of its best gags still revolved around subtle sound effects—the crunching of crackers, rattling of papers, and the explosive squelch of a can of tomatoes which Fields "opens" with a hatchet. This sequence, too, was repeated in "It's a Gift."

"So's Your Old Man," which followed, was a relatively short (sixty-seven-minute) feature film, with Fields playing the inventor of a shatterproof glass for automobiles. Richly embellished with sight gags, it was based on a *Redbook* magazine short story by Julian Street called "Mr. Bisbee's Princess," and concerned itself mainly with attempting to prove the efficacy of the invention. A typical scene showed Fields self-confidently heaving bricks at the "unbreakable" windshields of flivvers, unaware that his demonstration models have been moved and the windshields he is attacking so valiantly are decidedly un-shatterproof.

Fields' director was the gifted Gregory La Cava, who later became famous for "My Man Godfrey," then still a comparative newcomer to film. A former cartoonist, he tended to construct his films along the line of a comic strip, whether he was directing a semi-dramatic story such as "The New Schoolteacher" or a slapsticky Fields comedy. His talent was remarkable but always somewhat erratic and undisciplined, and his films stand the test of time less successfully than those of many of his contemporaries. He made one more silent with Fields, but unfortunately they never collaborated in the thirties, when both were at the peak of their powers. A pooling of their compatible insanities (ideally on "Million Dollar Legs," which sorely needed the bizarre inspirations of a La Cava) might have produced a masterpiece of the absurd. "So's Your Old Man" had the serene and graceful Alice Joyce as a notably off-beat leading lady opposite Fields—even though she played a princess. It was remade in the thirties as "You're Telling Me."

"The Potters," released early in 1927, would appear to be the most satisfying of all the silent Fields vehicles, although no known print exists today. It was based on a play by J. P. McEvoy, whose "Show Girl in Hollywood" and other stories were adapted into a number of highly successful pictures in the late twenties and early thirties. Its story-line was a simple one. Fields, the head of an average family, recklessly invests the family's entire bankroll, some four thousand dollars, in apparently worthless oil stock. Ultimately and quite by accident, the stock turns out to be worth a fortune, and Fields is a hero. (The same gimmick, with an orange grove instead of an oil well, was used later for "It's a Gift.")

Fred Newmeyer directed "The Potters." Although workmanlike, and responsible for many fast-moving two-reelers, he was not particularly creative, and it is significant that his only first-class comedies were those starring such major comedians as Harold Lloyd and W. C. Fields. Both performers always directed

The fire brigade has just left after a false alarm; "It's the Old Army Game." (Courtesy of Paramount Pictures)

their directors, whose functions sometimes were reduced to those of mechanics and efficiency. This was perhaps more fortunate for Lloyd, who, while he was not personally as funny as Fields, was a first-class organizer.

Some credit for the success of "The Potters" certainly must be allotted to screen writers Sam Mintz and Ray Harris, as well as to the charm of the original work, but the large measure we can assume belongs to Fields. Fields' performance, according to *The New York Times* and other journals, was restrained, subtle and natural. It was very much a broad comedy performance, allowing Fields bravura flights of frustration, fury and optimism, but from all accounts it was a disciplined concept, without the set routines that he liked to introduce for their own sake. This is the Fields silent film whose disappearance one most regrets today.

"Running Wild," likewise a 1927 release, reunited Fields with Gregory La Cava, and seems to have been less satisfactory than "The Potters." Once more Fields' self-discipline was in evidence, but the story was more contrived and not so sympathetic. Fields,·a hen-pecked milquetoast with a vicious family, allows himself to be hypnotized by a vaudeville magician. While under this spell he is metamorphosed into a leader of men, swinging a big deal for his firm that earns him not only a fat commission but respect from his abominable family and authority that keeps him top dog even after the hypnotic spell is broken.

However, the gradual humanizing of Fields through these pictures into less of a charlatan and more of a sympathetic family man was not made more plausible by his stubborn clinging to vaudeville costume and makeup—the large wide-winged collars, for example, and that reprehensible little moustache. Fields knew that the moustache was widely hated, which is probably why, in his perverse way, he insisted on keeping it. Yet the objectionable whisker consistently worked against him: as a family man, he lost sympathy through the ugly adornment, while as a con-man he lost credibility, since what hustler whose livelihood depended on ingratiating himself with the suckers would sport such an automatically alienating decoration?

"Running Wild" suffered more than most of his silents from the lack of dialogue, since the horrors of a nagging household and slovenly home had to be expressed in such obvious visual terms as having his wife sic the family dog on him. Fields unquestionably realized all the shortcomings; when he remade the film as a talkie, "The Man on the Flying Trapeze," the best laughs came from subtly underplayed lines of dialogue rather than from such elaborate visual routines as the one that provided the original film with its climax. Mary Brian, who played his daughter in "Running Wild," repeated the role in the re-make.

"Two Flaming Youths" took Fields out of suburban domesticity and restored him to the fairgrounds again. As Gabby Gilfoil, he was a conniving carnival operator, constantly on the run from creditors, sheriffs and unpaid landladies. It was a loosely put together comedy, agreeably unpredictable in the gags and routines, but Fields—or his films—was beginning to slip. The best story elements of "Two Flaming Youths" were later incorporated into the sound features "The Old Fashioned Way" and "You Can't Cheat an Honest Man."

"Two Flaming Youths" suffered from having been produced and directed by John Waters, one of Paramount's least talented film-makers. Waters came to earn the reputation of being able to turn out the worst film in any series to which he was assigned. Despite being given Gary Cooper, William Powell, a Zane Grey story and a liberal budget, he managed to turn the famous "Nevada" into a mediocre Western.

"Tillie's Punctured Romance," a 1928 re-make of an early and celebrated silent comedy, which followed, further hastened Fields' decline. It ran a mere fifty-seven minutes, and was produced independently in Hollywood by the Christie studio. Christie Comedies, which had been filled with bathing beauties and knock-about comics, had enjoyed a lively success in earlier days, but now their two-reelers were labored and old-fashioned and their stars usually second-raters. They could not compete with the much better short comedies from the Roach and Sennett studios, and survived only by virtue of their occasionally quite good fea-

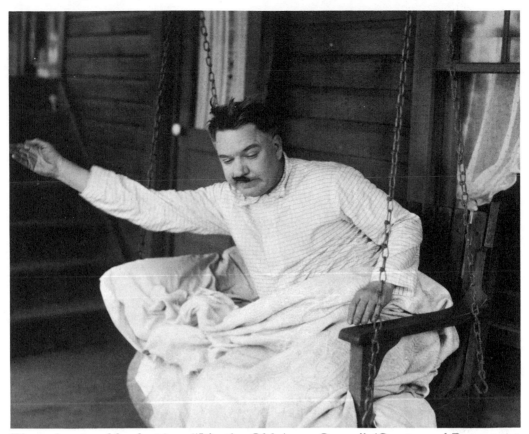

Elmer has trouble sleeping; "It's the Old Army Game." (Courtesy of Paramount Pictures)

ture comedies. These were now few and far between and did not compare with the really first-rate feature pictures, such as "So Long Letty," that Al Christie had made much earlier in the twenties.

"Tillie's Punctured Romance" was thought to be a sure-fire property capable of re-establishing the Christie name. It turned out instead to be the Christie nemesis, so poorly done that Paramount, which was distributing it, made no strong effort to sell it, and its exhibition life was a sorry one. Although it was supposedly based on the great Marie Dressler vehicle, the first feature-length film comedy that had served Mack Sennett so well in 1914, actually the principal characters were abstracted and thrust into a completely revamped scenario. Louise Fazenda played the old Marie Dressler role. But whereas the original "Tillie" had been lured away from the farm to the big city by the fortune-hunting slicker on a false promise of marriage, the new Tillie merely runs away from home to join the circus. Fields, as the conniving ringmaster, had the equivalent of the earlier Chaplin role. There any similarity ceased, and the film ended with some run-of-the-mill wartime slapstick—a vein that had been played to death in the twenties by Wallace Beery,

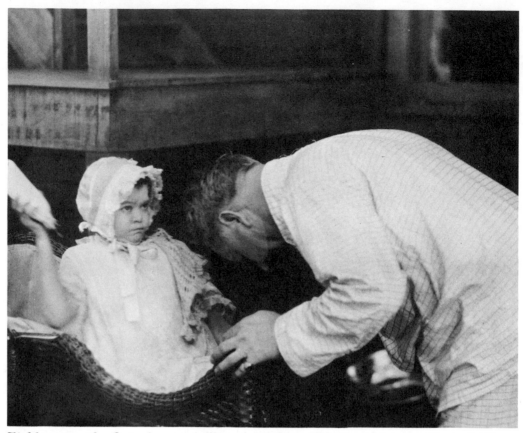

Fields meets the first of many belligerent babies; "It's the Old Army Game." (Courtesy of Paramount Pictures)

Raymond Hatton and other comedians following in the wake of Chaplin's "Shoulder Arms."

Since "Tillie" was presumably an expensive property to acquire, one wonders why Christie felt impelled to change and modernize it so extensively. The original "Tillie," though a historic and box office landmark, was too heavy-handed in its writing and direction (by Sennett himself) to achieve anything like the full potential offered by the story and situations. It had speed, lively slapstick, an all-star Sennett cast—and little else. Nevertheless, "Tillie" was such a huge success that a re-make was a sound idea. Putting Fields in the Chaplin role, even though it was an unsympathetic one, could have been an inspiration. The result, however, was disaster.

"Fools for Luck," Fields' final film for 1928, and his last silent, ran a bare sixty minutes and seemed to be the final nail hammered into his career as juggler, hustler, and ill-tempered *paterfamilias*. Incredibly, the plot was an unashamed reshuffling of the previous year's "The Potters," this time with Chester Conklin as the innocent investor in an apparently dry oil well, and Fields as the con man who

Elmer Prettywilly and son at picnic; "It's the Old Army Game." (Courtesy of Paramount Pictures)

bilks him. It was directed by Charles F. (Chuck) Reisner, one of the more skilled comedy directors of the twenties and an associate of Chaplin and Keaton. The screenplay writer, J. Walter Reuben, and the editor, George Nichols, Jr., went on to interesting directorial careers in the thirties. But all the talent behind the camera, and Fields with a lot of old and tried routines, including a poolroom episode, in front of the camera, couldn't save it.

"Fools for Luck" looked tired and uninspired, and neither the trade nor the daily press could get excited about it. Possibly Paramount hadn't tried too hard to help it; when a star's pictures have been slipping at the box office and his contract is up for renewal, it is an old dodge to deliberately make a "dog" with a weak script, a dull cast, and a slim budget. "Fools for Luck" had all of these, and whether by accident or design, it gave Paramount a perfectly reasonable excuse for not renewing Fields' contract.

He appears not to have been too upset by this turn of events. While he was a perennial worrier about financial security, he was important enough to expect offers from other film companies, or to go back to the stage. He announced

47

grandiose plans for returning to vaudeville and had his agent draw up several contracts. These plans apparently boosted his vanity and kept him amused, but he obviously had no intention of taking what would literally be a backward step. The clauses and conditions, the unreasonable billing and salary demands that he kept adding, on the whim of the moment or his latest drink, to these contractual negotiations were so unrealistic as to be almost fantastic.

Yet despite all of Fields' extravagant efforts to sabotage his career, he succeeded in foisting his impossible demands upon Earl Carroll, producer of an annual revue and girl show called "Earl Carroll's Vanities." It was during the run of this show that Fields exhibited, for a top Broadway ticket price, his vaudeville-trained talent for the underplayed ad-lib. One of the most fondly recalled examples occurred when a huge backdrop fell to the stage with a thunderous clatter, creating havoc but fortunately hurting no one.

"Mice!" muttered Fields petulantly, hardly turning around to witness the catastrophe.

It was also during his "Vanities" run that Fields perfected the hilarious golf routine that he had introduced earlier in a shorter version as the climax of "So's Your Old Man." Like his unforgettable pool table routine, it was a meticulously prepared essay in frustration. The golf ball never got hit. Carroll liked the "basic idea," but, true to his own milieu, suggested it might work better if pretty girls in bathing suits and a struggle with a fishing line were substituted for golf. Fields agreed amiably, and of course went on rehearsing his golf routine in secrecy. When he finally unveiled it, the audience was so prostrated with laughter that Carroll had to admit defeat. Fields used the golf routine *in toto* for his entry into the talkies in a two-reeler called "The Golf Specialist" made for RKO Radio in the spring of 1930.

Fields enjoyed his run in the "Vanities." Because he now "had it made" in a big Broadway show, besides having acquired the glamor of a movie star he basked in an aura of adulation and respect which he had not known in his vaudeville days. More secure now, he was correspondingly less aggressive, and his theatrical co-workers found him easier to get along with—though no less obstinate about getting his own way. For Fields, it was a relaxing and rewarding experience, but it was purely an interim.

Fields was not bitter about his frustrations and disappointments in movies, but he was unsatisfied, and anxious to prove himself. His difficulties with his East Coast filming had been exacerbated by a stock deal wherein he was severely trimmed by an apparently respectable but actually very shady New York banker. The fifty thousand dollars Fields lost turned into a splendid investment as a source of future comedy material and provided the inspiration for a whole succession of swindlers, such as the immortal J. Frothingham Waterbury of "The Bank Dick," who assures Fields in tones of mellow integrity: "I want to show you I'm honest in the worst way!"

Fields was ready to go back to the movies, and back to Hollywood. His taste for the warmth and laziness of the Hollywood scene had been sparked by working there in "Tillie's Punctured Romance," and obviously if he intended to carve a new career for himself in talkies, Hollywood was the place to be. Just past fifty, with two rich, full careers behind him, W. C. Fields' most creative years lay ahead.

Fields, Alice Joyce, and the first movie version of Fields' golf routine; "So's Your Old Man." (Courtesy of Paramount Pictures)

☞ **6.**

"The Golf Specialist"

Short subjects provided the ideal showcase for Fields' comedy talents. Most of his best material derived from vaudeville skits, and the twenty-minute format permitted an absolute concentration on Fields and nothing else. With no sub-plots or obligatory romantic interests to distract him, Fields could take his time, developing every little nuance, allowing himself the luxury of as many long pauses as he needed, pauses which in a feature-length film might well affect the overall pacing.

This is not to suggest that Fields was at a disadvantage in the full-length film, for his two finest works were features. "It's a Gift" (1934) was little more than three two-reelers, as methodically paced as Fields wanted them to be, linked by a slender thread of story. Conversely, his second masterpiece, 1940's "The Bank Dick," moved like lightning, its tangled web of sub-plots and bizarre characters never standing still long enough for any kind of routine to develop. But, just as Stan Laurel and Oliver Hardy made one or two superb features but still were to be seen at their best in two-reelers, so the most typical and undistilled Fields was to be found in shorts, although he turned out a grand total of only seven in his entire career.*

His first sound short, "The Golf Specialist" (made for RKO in 1930), disappoints as a piece of sustained comedy. It is a primitive two-reeler, typical of the early days of sound pictures when the camera was so often "nailed-down" and enclosed in a housing to keep its noise from reaching the mikes. Fields' great golfing routine was photographed as if being performed on a stage. All the flexibility and wide resources of film were thrown away. The patent cheapness of the production hardly matters; the stage entrances and exits, the phony backdrops to suggest plush hotel gardens and golf course, work well enough with the staginess of the whole, and it is the two genuine exteriors—a stock shot of a luxurious hotel, and a long shot of golfers on the links—that seem to be the intruders. However, the pacing of "The Golf Specialist" is resolutely that of the vaudeville stage rather than of the cinema: pauses last too long; the thrown-away line fails to register because the camera does not direct the eye to the speaker; details of by-play are missed when they could have been made clear by a closeup or skillful editing.

While one may argue that the stage performer does not have the benefit of cinematic tricks, he does have the advantage of physical presence and, in a sense, edits his own performance while directing audience attention as he goes along. "The Golf Specialist," therefore, is an accurate and complete recording of the content of Fields' skit—and for that we can be grateful—but, because he was performing for a static camera with techniques designed for an alive and responsive audience, it is hardly an accurate barometer of the laughs generated when Fields did it on the stage.

The skit opens by establishing that the burly house detective of a hotel has a flirtatious blonde wife. Her current interest, a mild little man, is spotted by the detective, who proceeds to twist his arms and legs around his neck and literally roll him out of the hotel. Enter an irate sailor looking for one Effington Bellweather who owes him money and has thus far successfully evaded him. The sailor dictates a furious and offensive note to the desk clerk, who promises to see that Mr. Bellweather gets it. No sooner has the sailor left than Mr. Bellweather arrives—Fields, still sporting that moustache, puffing on his cigar, twirling his cane, with a dapper straw hat on his head, and singing "Happy Days Are Here Again" in the cracked, rowdy Fieldsian tones.

He is given the letter, reads it with interest, and tears it to shreds. "Silly little girl," he murmurs, with a knowing wink at the clerk. Lighting a fresh cigar proves to be a problem. Matches don't work, nor does a lighter. He puts the lighter back in his pocket and searches for more matches. Belatedly, the lighter decides to function, blazing into life inside his pocket. An obnoxious little girl sidles up

---

* In later years, the sixteen- and eight-millimeter home movie market offered some short subjects bearing such titles as "Circus Slicker," "Hurry Hurry" and "The Great Chase," but these were excerpts culled from Fields' Universal features, and mainly showed the slapstick chase climaxes.

52

W. C. Fields as Samuel Bisbee in "So's Your Old Man." (Courtesy of Paramount Pictures)

Fields as "Pa" Potter; "The Potters." (Courtesy of Paramount Pictures)

Fields as the browbeaten office clerk in "Running Wild." (Courtesy of Paramount Pictures)

Fields suffers from nagging wife (Marie Shotwell) and lazy son (Barney Raskle); "Running Wild." (Courtesy of Paramount Pictures)

to him, shaking her money box. Against his better judgment, Fields tries to be pleasant. He invites her to sing a song for him and asks how old she is. The brat tells him that she's five, and that she'll sing a song only if he gives her a dollar.

"You're more than five!" he growls, and refuses to give her the dollar. "I don't care," she sneers back at him, shaking her money box. "I've got more than fifty dollars in here." Looking around carefully to make sure that the lobby is deserted, he makes a grab for the money box, but she fights back like a demon. Her screams bring other guests to the scene, and Fields starts to stroke her hair soothingly. "Probably has a pin sticking in her," he explains. Hoping for a later try at the money box, he continues to stroke her hair, but she moves away from under his hand, and her place is taken by the house-detective's blonde wife, who has a fox fur hanging down her back. Babbling incoherently to no one in particular about the little girl and how charming she is, Fields madly fondles the fox fur. The house detective, discovering Fields apparently patting his wife's derrière, moves in for the attack. The wife convinces him of their innocence, however, and for the time being he withdraws.

Fields, contrite and gallant, strikes up an acquaintance with the willing blonde, though his first overtures are delayed somewhat while he searches for his hat, which has somehow perched on top of his cane. The wife tells him her tale of woe, what a brute of a husband she has and how he is always beating her. Fields is aghast. "Why, I've never struck a woman in my whole life," he tells her proudly, "not even my own mother!" While they are talking, the brat returns to place a toy dog beside Fields' leg, just in time for the hotel gardener to spray Fields while watering the flowers. With a mighty curse, Fields kicks the dog out of his way—a piece of business on which Fields knew many variations—and suggests that his new companion might like to join him in a game of golf. She is willing, though admitting that she doesn't even know which end of the caddy to hit.

Fields' caddy is a wizened little wreck of a man wearing a gigantic cap and shoes with large holes in them. He hands Fields a club apparently made of rubber, for it promptly twists out of shape. "Wrong club," murmurs Fields. "Try this putting niblick," suggests the caddy, offering a new club. Fields is fascinated by the sound of the phrase, repeats the words "putting niblick" several times to get the feel of them, and then explains to his lady companion: "The little fellow obviously doesn't understand the nomenclature of the game." Fields seems to be having trouble getting his game started. His hat falls off repeatedly; one club wraps itself around his neck like a corkscrew and is rejected—"The shaft is warped"— and other golfers inconsiderately shout "Fore." When their ball lands near Fields, he promptly pockets it and goes on with his own efforts.

The caddy, however, is still preventing Fields from taking that first vital stroke. The caddy takes out a mysterious package, unwraps layers of thin and crackling tissue paper, and removes a pie. Fields waits patiently for a while and then again takes up his stance. The caddy now tidily gathers up the disarrayed tissue

Fields, as Gabby Gilfoil, tries to lure sheriff (Chester Conklin) into shell game;
"Two Flaming Youths." (Courtesy of Paramount Pictures)

Fields with Chester Conklin; a publicity still for "Tillie's Punctured Romance."
(Courtesy of Paramount Pictures)

paper and, with more crackling, neatly folds it into a small square. Fields takes time out to comment: "Imagine bringing a pie to the golf course. A pint, yes, but a pie, never!" The absurdity intrigues him, but he can't quite find the simile he is looking for. "It's like carrying something or other to somewhere," he mutters, ". . . as the case may be. . . ." Then he steps on the tissue paper, which attaches itself to his feet, his golf-club and his hands. A good deal of his fast disappearing patience is required to remove it.

At last Fields is in position to swing again; but now the caddy moves into range once more, and somehow, in a matter of seconds, his shoes have developed a squeak that sounds like an army of giant marching rats. The noise reminds Fields of a similar experience some years ago when some golfer friends of his were kicked to death by a canary. He never does finish this anecdote, for in bending over to oil the caddy's offending shoes, he plants his own foot square in the middle of the very squishy pie. No sooner has the pie been laboriously removed from his foot than it inevitably becomes attached to the club. Fields is fast approaching a stage of violent rage toward his unhelpful caddy.

"I'd like to wring your neck," he threatens. "I'd like to wash it first and give it a good wring!" The gooey pie, mixed up now with remnants of tattered tissue paper, is everywhere. As Fields tries to restore order, he murmurs contrite apologies to his lady friend. "This is really disgusting . . . I'm sorry you had to see this." Spitting out tissue paper which somehow has got in his mouth, he becomes further enraged by his caddy, whom he had ordered to stand perfectly still but who is wriggling two exposed toes. Unable to stand the torment any longer, Fields clobbers the offending toes a mighty whack with his club.

There is a brief cutaway to the hotel lobby, where a Federal man is conferring with the house detective. He has a "Wanted" poster for the elusive Mr. Bellweather, who is sought by the police for a number of heinous crimes which are shown to include, as the camera pans down the lengthy and detailed poster, such misdemeanors as eating spaghetti in public, posing as the Prince of Wales, and revealing the facts of life to an Indian.

Back on the golf course, Fields—at last ready to take his first stroke—is delayed once more when a handsome lady in riding breeches wanders across his field of play, pausing for a moment to remark, "I forgot something!"

"Probably her horse," Fields complains between gritted teeth; whatever it is, she decides it doesn't matter, and starts away, rather carelessly stepping on Fields' club and breaking it in two. Magnanimously, he gives the club to his caddy— "for short holes"—and now turns his attention to a second lady who has invaded his domain to take her large afghan hound for a stroll. "What a beautiful camel!" he comments. Having chosen a new club, Fields now would be ready to swing, were it not that the caddy has plonked his foot squarely in the middle of Fields' straw hat, removing the top entirely. "I'll have to have it re-blocked," Fields remarks with admirable self-control, and then snarls a sarcastic "Thanks!" to the hapless caddy.

W. C. Fields as circus ring-master in re-make of "Tillie's Punctured Romance."
(Courtesy of Paramount Pictures)

The house detective's wife, still waiting demurely and with patience, is now surely to be given a demonstration of the game. Fields begins his swing—and the caddy tears a strip of paper with the sound of ripping fabric. Fields gingerly feels his nether regions, but can discover no damage to his trousers or his dignity. Another tentative swing—and more ominous rips. Just as Fields launches his first successful swing, the sheriff bursts into the scene; the golf club connects with the lawman's rifle, which discharges into the air, bringing down a fine goose. Unruffled, Fields continues explaining to his lady pupil that the secret of successful golfing lies in keeping the wrists close together. It is a convenient stance for the sheriff, who obligingly snaps the handcuffs on. Attempting to ignore both the sheriff and the handcuffs, Fields is led away, repeating over and over that one essential rule, "Keep the wrists close together. . . ."

Supporting Marilyn Miller, not even given billing on the still captions, in "Her Majesty Love." (Courtesy of Warner Brothers)

☞ 7.

Hollywood and the Talkies

Fields' arrival back in Hollywood in 1931 took the form of a typical movie "entrance" which oddly enough he never recreated in any of his films. Driving in out of the desert, he summoned flunkeys to act as porters for his considerable luggage, and strode toward the hotel's reception desk like a Great White Hunter, his safari in tow. In lordly tones he demanded the bridal suite. The receptionist, mildly taken aback, timidly pointed out that the bridal suite was traditionally reserved for married couples, and usually newlyweds. His *savoir-faire* shattered not one whit, Fields announced that he'd take a look around town and bring a bride back with him. The initial entrance may possibly have been suggested to Fields by Groucho Marx' famous arrival in "Animal Crackers," but the punch line was solely his own.

Fields was happy to be in Hollywood. Many of his friends were there now —directors Gregory La Cava and Eddie Sutherland among them—and he felt ready to tackle the movies seriously. New York and the stage were behind him; so was a long cross-country trek by automobile which was to provide fodder for many a future movie.

Aware that his past movie career was hardly a spectacular success, Fields felt optimistic about the new medium of sound, and the bank crashes of '29 were now well behind him—having affected him far less severely than he liked people to believe. Early impressions of Hollywood in any case were conducive to optimism. The sun was bright, the air—in those days—was fresh and permanently intermingled with the scent of tropical plants; the green lawns and shrubbery were always sparkling and freshly bathed from early-morning sprinklers; the girls striding along Hollywood Boulevard were pretty and abundantly healthy, as though living on a steady diet of fresh air and orange juice; and far from least, Hollywood is the only place in America where the eateries—from humble diner to plush nightclub—serve your food exactly as ordered, eggs well done if so stipulated, toast lightly browned as though fussed over by an art director. (The reason may be less a desire to serve than the fear of reprisals from important customers, but the result is uncommonly good service.)

Enthusiasm and optimism are automatic by-products of the initial days in Hollywood, and the trick is to cash in on that optimism and get down to work before the sweet smell of the tropical plants turn sickly and the dry heat becomes enervating rather than stimulating. Fields' own sense of well-being was not matched by a corresponding benevolence from the studios. It was not a good time for a silent comedian with a spotty box-office record to present himself in Hollywood. Such previous top-liners as Buster Keaton and Harry Langdon already were having very tough sledding. Ben Turpin, Karl Dane and other favorites from the slapstick silents were reduced to bit roles in features and serials, and occasional leads in shorts that made stiff and unsuccessful attempts to recreate their former comedy styles. Raymond Griffith, the sophisticated top-hat comedian of the twenties, was out as a performer—not because his voice was no good, but because he literally had no voice at all, a speech impediment making it impossible for him to speak much above a whisper. He made a couple of two-reelers in sound, playing a man with a bad cold, and then moved to the production side of the business.

Chaplin and Lloyd, with their own companies, were holding their own; so were Laurel and Hardy and Charlie Chase. For the rest, comedy was in the hands of such sophisticated directors as Lubitsch and Harry D'Arrast, and stage performers like the Marx Brothers, Wheeler and Woolsey, Joe E. Brown and Jimmy Durante, who had sprung to overnight popularity in films with the coming of sound. Producers showed more interest in new faces from vaudeville like Clark and McCullough than in Fields, a vaudeville headliner and a known film name. But he was having a difficult time for that prime old Hollywood reason—you're only as good as your last picture. Moreover, star status counted far more in Hollywood than it had in the East, so he could hardly be blamed for reluctance to start from scratch in lesser roles and work his way to the top again. Yet that was what he virtually was forced to do.

62

The Continental-flavored musical comedies so popular in the early days of sound were coming to the end of their vogue. But one of them, "Her Majesty Love," starring Marilyn Miller and Ben Lyon, had a key role that suited Fields as if it were made for him. Although his first scene did not occur until twenty-five minutes into the seventy-five-minute picture, and the part thereafter was a supporting one, it was a good part, and, even more important, it offered Fields chances to infiltrate his specialties once he set foot on the sound stage. Had the film, which was based on a German original and retained the German locale, been played as straight drama, the Fields role might even have provided an outlet for the self-indulgent histrionics of the great Emil Jannings.

But Fields saw it for what it was—schnapps and beer instead of scotch and rye, and "Herr Toerrek" as Eustace McGargle with a German accent. Fields made a valiant attempt at a guttural German accent in his first scenes. Either he found it got in his way too much, or director William Dieterle, himself a German, discovered it was eating up too much production time to coax the accent out of Fields for each shot, and gave up the battle. In any event, since both hero and heroine were uncompromisingly American in every tone and inflection, regardless of the "von" attached to the hero's name, the need for Fields to struggle with the German accent dwindled as the film progressed. Fields dropped the accent, and concentrated on juggling instead. McGargle was back, and to stay.

Even without Fields, "Her Majesty Love" would have been a charming piece of frou-frou. William Dieterle, a prominent German actor of the twenties, who had come to America to star in and direct German versions of Hollywood films,* began directing American films in 1931. Although his subsequent career was uneven, he contributed many films of note and permanent value to the movie scene of the thirties and forties, among them the Zola and Pasteur biographies with Paul Muni, the much underrated "The Last Flight," and most important of all, "The Devil and Daniel Webster," a classic of Americana.

Dieterle's handling of "Her Majesty Love" was lively and visual; the camera fluid and mobile at a time when many directors were still shooting static stage set-ups; the pacing fast, and the cutting decidedly inventive. One particularly exciting transition showed the harried hero disgustedly sitting at his desk and suddenly tossing into the air all of the white papers and correspondence by which he is trapped. As the white sheets flutter downwards, they dissolve into the white wings of flying doves—and we are in Venice. Exposition, explanations and time lapses are all thrown away as unnecessary by this one brilliant dissolve. It passed

*   When sound came in, Hollywood saw itself losing the vast European market because of the language barrier. The simpler expedients of dubbing and subtitling would come later, but initially the studios tried to solve the problem by shooting two or three separate versions of their bigger pictures. The original script would be followed and the same sets used, but German and French actors (France and Germany being two key markets) would replace the American stars and European directors be brought in to make these foreign versions. In some cases the radically different style of a European director could result in a completely different (and often superior) version of a given film. Among the films Dieterle directed was the German version of "Moby Dick," in which he substituted for John Barrymore as Captain Ahab.

unnoticed, yet when William Wyler used the same device, and in the same context, in his considerably later "Dodsworth" (a prestige film that the critics presumably could allow themselves to take more seriously) it was acclaimed as a master stroke! Articles on film technique still attribute this exhilarating moment solely to Wyler.

"Her Majesty Love" is full of such pleasing images. The film gets under way with a wild cabaret sequence in which the heroine is introduced in novel fashion by appearing from behind a screenful of gradually popping balloons. Dieterle obviously liked the effect, for he used it again a few years later for his introductory shot of Bette Davis in an exceptionally good melodrama, "Fog Over Frisco."

The plot of "Her Majesty Love" is that standby of romantic musical comedy (especially when of German or Austrian origin) the rough and misunderstanding-strewn path to happiness of a playboy with family "responsibilities" and the socially unacceptable barmaid whom he loves. Ben Lyon was the businessman-playboy hero, an executive in the ballbearing factory owned by his family. Marilyn Miller was the girl who was required to live down not only the disgrace of being a barmaid (although that oft-repeated word seemed hardly to apply to her job in the lavish cabaret where she worked), but also the stigma of having a decidedly unpolished vaudeville juggler as her father! Currently out of show business, the father gets occasional employment as a barber, also not likely to enhance his social standing.

Much of the early comedy byplay in the picture has a decidedly Fieldsian air to it, as though the Great Man had dropped a few hints here and there. At a stuffy board meeting, perennial movie grouch Clarence Wilson noisily cracks walnuts and complains that he hasn't had his coffee yet; when it is finally delivered, his pince-nez promptly falls into it. Only when Fields enters the plot, however, does its comedy content soar. He is in bed, asleep, when his daughter calls him on the telephone to announce her engagement. Fussily putting on his glasses before he answers the phone, he proves to be less impressed by the happy news than he is by the novelty of speaking to his prospective son-in-law.

"First time I've ever been called Father by a strange man," he muses while he makes a major chore out of pulling on his gloves; he then goes out into the pouring rain to sit in the unprotected rumble seat of a car which will take him to a swank buffet party to meet his new in-laws. The sequence which follows, in which the very social von Wellingens gradually become aware, to their consternation, of the kind of family that is soon to be allied with theirs, turns out to be something of a blueprint for the engagement party that the American socialites, the Bel Goodies, will throw for Fields' daughter in his much later "You Can't Cheat an Honest Man."

Fields enters the lion's den without any major disaster occurring, his amiable good nature apparently offsetting his far-from-fashionable clothing. Fred von

Wellingen (Ben Lyon) makes an official announcement of his engagement to Fields' daughter Lia (Marilyn Miller), and the statement obviously doesn't sit well with one of the elder von Wellingens, who indicates that the situation may well change, though he adds that things can go on as they are ". . . for the present."

Fields, having heard only the last few words, brightens up. "Oh, am I going to get a present?" he beams amiably, and then when he sees that this is not the case, snarls, "*Keep it!*"

Unimpressed by the stuffed-shirt von Wellingens, he circulates among the guests, trying to make friends. His generous offers of free haircuts to all comers do not meet with an overwhelming response, nor does his instruction to a waiter, "Hot cheese for the gentleman!" offered in a polite effort to cover up a guest's noisy sneeze.

Such remnants of society composure as he has left intact are soon shattered when Fields heaves some chocolate eclairs to a diner at the far end of the table, and decides to become the complete life of the party by performing his juggling act. Amidst howls of protest from thoroughly frightened dowagers, the wild man is firmly asked to leave—which he does, but not before adding insult to injury by tipping the butler and engaging in a complicated bit of exit business with an umbrella.

An attempt is made to save the day for his daughter, but by now she is more angry than embarrassed. "You can go to hell!" she forthrightly tells the dignified assemblage, sends a food-laden table crashing on its side, and storms out in a fury.

With the love story temporarily at a standstill, a secondary plot appears in the person of Leon Errol as a much-married and lecherous baron. Errol, like Fields, had been a big name in the theatrical world, a stage star on Broadway for years, though never important in silent films. Although he was never to approach the stature of Fields as a star of sound films, Errol achieved a considerable measure of success as a star of two-reel comedies, the "Mexican Spitfire" series, and many feature comedies involving marital mixups and dual roles, in the late thirties and early forties. While many of his stage tricks are well employed in "Her Majesty Love," and he manages, in his scenes with Fields, to invest his unsympathetic character with a touching pathos, he invariably winds up as the straight man.

Anxious to make Marilyn Miller his next bride, he applies to Fields for permission to go a-courting. "Granted," murmurs Fields, and proceeds to tell his daughter what an advantageous match it will be. "He's rich and old. What more do you want? You can look forward to a happy widowhood!" Errol begins his courtship, and he and Fields make the most of a rather flimsy routine in which Errol is constantly having his flunkies deliver bouquets of flowers to his beloved, while Fields, believing them to be from von Wellingen and not wanting them to upset the new courtship plans, repeatedly throws them out of the window where they land back at the feet of the bemused Errol. Ultimately, Errol delivers the flowers in person, strapped to his wrist. It's a mild bit, but the facial miming and interplay between Fields and Errol give the trifle a comic stature it hardly deserves.

Fields' daughter, disillusioned in love, is prepared to go along with the marriage of convenience, and the wedding is performed in a matter-of-fact manner at the Marriage Bureau, where the baron is an old and familiar client. After the ceremony he takes his young bride to the cabaret for a wedding supper at which much of the dialogue has the raw and uninhibited "blue" quality of many sex farces in this pre-censorship era. Hoping to ply his bride with foods which will arouse her thus far undemonstrated passionate nature, Errol enlists the aid of an understanding waiter, who suggests pointedly that "oysters are excellent for raising an appetite," and volunteers the information that "these oysters have been in some of the world's finest beds." Errol, carrying the *double-entendre* to more obvious extremes, asks her, "Don't you feel like a little goose?" By now Marilyn is firmly convinced that her marriage is a mistake, and wants only to be reunited with Fred, who is waiting in the wings after arriving seconds too late to prevent the wedding. The baron takes the shock philosophically, for the pursuit of young brides is his life's work, and he can soon find a successor. He agrees to a divorce, leaving Marilyn a baroness and thus able to live up to the social requirements of Fred's family—even though he has made it clear by now that he is prepared to marry her even if it means renouncing his family and the wealth that goes with it.

Fields tends to fade out of the climactic sections of "Her Majesty Love." His big scenes are to be found in the middle where they happily offset the conventional boy-meets-girl, boy-loses-girl musical comedy story. Yet, although the film hardly exploits his talents to a degree approaching their powers, it was sufficient to re-establish him in movies and garner for him the critical acclaim necessary to launch his second career in films.

The other players fared less well. It would be a long time before Leon Errol attained his moderate success in sound films, while Ford Sterling—a popular actor if never a major one in silents, made no impact at all in the talkies. The enormously popular musical comedy star Marilyn Miller never caught on as a screen personality, despite ambitious attempts to "sell" her through the medium of a movie version of one of her biggest stage successes, "Sally"—with a score by Jerome Kern. Her charming personality and infectious gaiety were so rooted in the techniques of the stage—designed to reach the back row of the balcony—that on screen they seemed stiff and artificial. Even her sunny smile had the quality of an exaggerated and over-used affectation.

Conversely, Ben Lyon, whose excellent speaking voice made him much in demand in the early talkies, never attained the front-rank stardom that his good looks, personality and acting ability seemed to warrant. At a time when screen leading men fell roughly into two camps, the suave gentlemen (Barrymore, Arliss, Menjou) and the aggressive roughnecks and smart alecks (Cagney, Gable, Lee Tracy), his smooth and polished self-confidence was a few years ahead of the public acceptance of such types. When Robert Taylor, Robert Montgomery and a romanticized Gable brought the type very much into vogue in the mid-thirties, it was too late to help Ben Lyon, whose acting career dwindled into "B" pictures. Only Fields and Dieterle benefited noticeably from "Her Majesty Love." Seen today, it holds up as a sporadically charming and amusing film, very typical of the Continental-flavored musical comedy of its period and rather above average for its genre. Principally it is of more interest academically than as entertainment because of its importance as a stepping-stone in the careers of director Dieterle and comedian Fields.

Fields as the President of Klopstokia; "Million Dollar Legs." (Courtesy of Paramount Pictures)

☞ 8.

A New Image at Paramount

It makes a good story, as told in Taylor's biography,* for Mack Sennett to imply that he really put Fields on his talkie feet with the four shorts they made together, and that when Paramount made Fields a better offer, Sennett gracefully stepped aside. But the facts are otherwise. Paramount came to Fields offering a deal before Sennett did, and two films under Fields' new contract with Paramount were completed before the first of the Sennett shorts was made. However, it is fair to say that the success of the Sennett shorts eventually influenced Paramount in giving Fields a much freer hand than before with his features. More importantly, the four Sennett shorts ("The Dentist," "The Fatal Glass of Beer," "The Pharmacist" and "The Barber Shop") enabled Fields to polish his film technique and become more familiar with the microphone. The Paramount executives, unsure of how to use Fields, were not giving him the opportunity to ex-

* W. C. Fields, His Follies and Fortunes by Robert Lewis Taylor; Doubleday, 1949.

periment and to feel his way around in the first pictures he made for them. Their feeling seemed to be that Fields could not sustain a full-length feature on his own. Thus his first few films varied between placing him in "star" parts in which he was off-screen much of the time, other players getting most of the footage, and what amounted to interpolations, his specialty routines appearing like short subjects which had been dumped arbitrarily into unrelated pictures.

His first feature under the new Paramount contract was "Million Dollar Legs," which was released in the summer of 1932. Based on an original story by Joseph L. Mankiewicz, it was a somewhat disorganized mixture of farce, satire and imitation Sennett slapstick. Fields is the President of Klopstokia, a bankrupt country ridden by intrigue and perpetually on the verge of revolution, its only asset being that practically every member of the populace is an athletic superman. Since this is Olympics year in the United States, Klopstokia is counting on restoring its national prestige and fortunes by winning all the events. The film was short enough (a mere sixty-four minutes) and sufficiently zany and unpredictable to be constantly entertaining, but it suffered from the lack of a consistent style. In the final analysis it looked like an elongated version of one of Sennett's similarly disconnected two-reelers of the twenties.

1933's Marx Brothers' "Duck Soup," with a somewhat similar plot-line, was far more successful because of its discipline and the consistency shown in keeping its insanities within the boundaries of a comic-opera framework. Curiously, however, the reputation of "Million Dollar Legs" grew through the years. Perhaps because it was made during a period when there was relatively little sight-gag humor (and certainly too much talk) in the American film, it came to be hailed as a comic masterpiece and a refreshing breaking away from tradition. In similar fashion the unconventional Lester/Beatles films of the sixties were acclaimed for a "new" style which was really no style at all but an amalgamation of many existing ones. The use of the title "Million Dollar Legs" for another film later in the thirties (not a remake) gave the critics yet another chance to laud the old "masterpiece," and now one even finds it discussed as a piece of "American dadaism." It is a perfect example of how a reputation can be inflated.

Audiences are not so easily taken in, however, and while the film, which is undeniably funny, gets its just allowance of laughs and audience response, it rarely gets the sustained climactic applause that so deservedly greets the end of the genuine Fields classics when they make periodic reappearances.

No one element of "Million Dollar Legs" really dominates the picture, though the elaborate sight-gag spoofs in which black-cloaked Ruritanian spies rise on hydraulic elevators from underground hideouts in woodland glades perhaps are most memorable. Lyda Roberti as the sexy spy, Mata Machree, who uses her wiles on the Olympic team in an effort to sabotage their athletic virility is quite marvelous in one of the few roles that ever did justice to her vivacity and sense of fun. Susan Fleming, the incredibly lovely if somewhat colorless heroine, has her blandness utilized rather cunningly by director Eddie Cline. At

Jack Oakie, Susan Fleming, Fields, Syd Saylor, Lyda Roberti, Hugh Herbert, Billy Gilbert; "Million Dollar Legs." (Courtesy of Paramount Pictures)

one point she informs her American boy friend, Jack Oakie, that all Klopstokian girls are named Angela. "Why?" inquires Oakie, reasonably. "Why not?" she replies, with equal reasonableness and without any credit being afforded Lewis Carroll. She then suggests that he sing her the Klopstokian Love Song, which is printed on goatskin parchment. This turns out to be a double-talk version of the lovely title song from Maurice Chevalier's "One Hour With You."

Fields puts in occasional appearances at his Presidential councils, which usually are climaxed by a test of strength between him and his Secretary of the Treasury, played by Hugh Herbert. All matters of state are pushed aside as they clear the conference table for a bout of Indian wrestling. "Next time!" promises the exhausted Herbert as his arm is rapidly pushed down to the table.

Their final confrontation takes place in Los Angeles' Olympic arena, where Mata Machree's sexy gyrations inspire Hugh Herbert to unprecedented feats of strength. Temporarily he is ahead, but both he and Mata Machree are exhausted. "I bane done all I can do—in public," she gasps.

Fields also is too exhausted to be rallied for a final effort. "Get him mad!"

The President of Klopstokia (Fields) and Secretary of the Treasury (Hugh Herbert) in conference; "Million Dollar Legs." (Courtesy of Paramount Pictures)

advises daughter Angela, and Jack Oakie proceeds to lambaste him with insults. "You're right," agrees Fields, wiping perspiration from his neck, too low in spirit to be aroused. One particularly horrendous insult produces a brief rise in the Fields temperature, but the anger passes, and Fields remains limp. Then, accidentally, Oakie causes a five-hundred-pound weight to fall on Fields' toe. With a cry of outrage and pain, Fields grabs the weight and flings it after the fleeing Oakie, winning not only the weight-lifting contest but the shot-put as well, and wrapping up the Olympics for Klopstokia. It is an amusing gag, but hardly a strong climax to a movie which really has no climax but seems to finish when the film—and the inspiration—runs out.

Fields was better served in his second picture for Paramount, "If I Had a Million," though this is another movie that saw its reputation grow with the years, largely due to that part of it in which Fields appears. A collection of episodes written and directed by various top-ranking talents, it is motivated—and the stories linked—by a framing story in which a dying millionaire, well played by Richard Bennett, decides to give all his money away to strangers rather than let it fall into the hands of his grasping and quite undeserving relatives.

His method is to take an eye-dropper and select names at random from the phone book. (The first name picked out by the eye-dropper turns out to be that of John D. Rockefeller, and is passed by.) To each person thus chosen, a million dollars is given, and, conveniently, each recipient has a personal story that fits into a neatly defined category of comedy, pathos, tragedy or drama. Thus hunted crook George Raft cannot cash the check to obtain the money that would enable him to make a getaway. May Robson uses the money to buy up the cheerless old ladies' home in which she lives. Convicted murderer Gene Raymond learns of the windfall too late for it to help him in financing a new trial and goes screaming to the electric chair. In the justly famous pantomimic vignette directed by Ernst Lubitsch, Charles Laughton, a downtrodden office clerk, finds the check in his morning mail; he calmly leaves his desk, walks through a maze of corridors and outer offices into the inner sanctum of the company president, blows him a raucous razzberry, and turns on his heel toward a life of ease and retirement. At the film's end, comedy and happy endings have out-balanced tragedy, and even the stricken millionaire, having found a new lease on life through bringing happiness to others, runs away from business conferences to enjoy home-made apple pies at the old ladies' home!

For a film that, through the years, has become almost legendary, "If I Had a Million" created remarkably little stir when it was first released. Not even given a first run in many cities, it was handled by Paramount as a second feature. Neither reviewers nor audiences were greatly entranced. As an all-star film it failed to generate the same enthusiasm as had "Grand Hotel," and in general it was regarded as little more than a group of shorts strung together. Such praise as it did garner was usually for imaginativeness in creating a new structure for film, but it was not thought that such a structure could be useful for more than an occasional novelty.

Of course, the high standard of shorts in those days, and the great number of them (dramatic and musical as well as comedy), makes this attitude a little easier to understand. Too, all-star films had been fairly common since the big musical revue films of 1929, and "If I Had a Million" lacked the really big Paramount stars of the period—Maurice Chevalier, Jeanette MacDonald, Marlene Dietrich, Nancy Carroll, Fredric March, Kay Francis. In terms of contemporary box-office values, Gary Cooper was the only major name in the picture. Still, it was such an expertly made film and such an entertaining one that it is difficult to see why it did not become a much bigger hit. Paramount could not have been too concerned, as it must have been economical to make. Most of the players, writers and directors—a fantastic overall roster of talent—were under contract. Each sequence had its own director and crew, and probably was shot quite quickly. Even as a second feature, it undoubtedly brought back a healthy profit, while in Europe it was treated as a major release and benefited from enthusiastic critical acclaim.

In later years the reputation of "If I had a Million" developed through word-of-mouth. In Europe it was withdrawn from release fairly early, and in the United States it never seems to have been reissued in its complete form. Sequences were

A blind man gag deleted from the final version of "If I Had a Million." (Courtesy of Paramount Pictures)

trimmed; the grim Gene Raymond sequence was removed entirely, as was the wry episode in which prostitute Wynne Gibson celebrates her good fortune by sleeping alone in a luxurious hotel bedroom, settling down in the sheets only to arise again with a start, remove her stockings, and return to bed and, presumably, a new life. The Gibson sequence is still the first one to be cut for United States television exposure. This and the May Robson–old ladies' home episode, both directed by veteran James Cruze, represent some kind of triumph for the use of silent technique in the sound film. The most famous sequence of all, Fields' road hog episode, funny though it is, now seems to have been overrated.

Drivers whom he viewed as road hogs had always irked Fields, especially so since an incident on Long Island when a brash Negro driver had the temerity to overtake Fields, who was bowling along merrily in his new Cadillac with Will Rogers and Chic Sale. Determined to overtake the upstart, Fields succeeded only in totally wrecking his car and landing Will Rogers in the hospital. The plot of his segment of "If I Had a Million" must have delighted his vengeful heart.

He and wife Alison Skipworth have skimped and saved to buy a new road-

Fields, with Alison Skipworth, in "If I Had a Million." (Courtesy of Paramount Pictures)

ster; just as they are taking it away from the automobile sales room, their new car is wrecked by one of these abominable drivers. The timely arrival of Richard Bennett's million-dollar check rescues them from despair and suggests a unique revenge. Buying a fleet of jalopies and placing husky drivers at the helms, Fields and Skipworth take to the roads, Fields riding majestically at the head of their caravan, scanning the distant horizon like a Seventh Cavalry officer looking for Apaches. Let one imprudent motorist scrape a fender or occupy more than his fair share of the center of the road and, at a signal, one of Fields' motorized army takes after him, never giving up until the miscreant's car is a thorough wreck.

In theory, and with Fields leading the fray, it sounds as if it could not fail, but alas! this fine idea never lives up to expectations. Norman Taurog, an expert at gentler comedy, seems unwilling to give the sequence the vicious bite it needs. The car chases and wrecks are funny, as are the casual dismissals of the car-wreckers, with a bonus, when they have performed their duties. But there is little variety in the methods by which the offending cars are chased and disposed of, and the sequence lacks cumulative effect. The final confrontation is hardly a climax, more a repetition. (Taurog would have done well to study the silent Laurel and Hardy classic "Two Tars," in which autos are steadily wrecked in a steadily building crescendo of fury and frenzy.)

Even the Fields dialogue and his exchange of florid compliments with the ample Miss Skipworth seem forced and lacking in his customary sparkle, although the sheer, delightful, demoniacal inspiration of the sequence may well have captivated audiences as yet unfamiliar with the content. Unlike most such Fields set-pieces, this famous episode diminishes in value with repeated viewings.

The best episode in "If I Had a Million" takes place early in the proceedings and never is referred to by critics or historians. This is the brilliant Charlie Ruggles-Mary Boland episode, so smoothly and tastefully handled by that under-rated master of sophistication and charm, William Seiter. Ruggles is a rabbit-fancier, and also a henpecked husband. His wife's nagging invades his leisure hours, so that a nightly trip to the bathroom for temporary escape has become a matter of routine. She invades his sleep too, in nightmarish, surrealistic dreams. His nervousness is an occupational hazard, since he works in a china store, and the casualties in bric-a-brac and vases are regularly deducted from his downward spiraling paycheck. With the advent of the million dollars, he puts his wife (lovingly) in her place, takes his pet rabbit on an elaborate leash to the china store and systematically breaks everything in sight in full view of his pompous and tyrannical employer—who of course is unaware that the damage can be paid for.

The sequence is a pure delight and a tour-de-force for Charlie Ruggles, although one can easily envision Fields having a wonderful time with this episode, too. A generally high standard is maintained in all of the sequences, the single exception being the Gary Cooper story, which is disappointingly trivial and lacking in real humor and has the further disadvantage of emphasizing its triteness by coming close to the end of the film on the heels of so much superior material. On the whole, however, "If I Had a Million" is probably the best of those films that were composed of several different stories, and certainly better in every way than "On Our Merry Way," "Tales of Manhattan" and other films that employed a similar form but with far less legitimate framing stories.

While both "If I Had a Million" and "Million Dollar Legs" were disappointing in the Fields comedy that they generated, they are important in that they set up the basic Fields character for all the films to come. Eustace McGargle of course remained the bedrock of all Fields' work, but the added subtleties and greater warmth began with these first two Paramount talkies. For one thing, Fields' physical appearance was changed; the revolting little moustache, still retained in "Her Majesty Love," now had gone for good. The snappy straw hats and boaters which had characterized the earlier Fields as a dapper man-about-town, even if a frustrated one, were replaced by a battered top hat, signifying a lost dignity and automatically classifying the new Fields as more victim than aggressor. In both 1932 films he was cast as a family man, father in one, husband in the other. And in both films his various anti-social aggressions were justified by previous actions taken against him. It still would be a year or two before Fields would hit his full stride, or before he could productively ride roughshod over front offices, scripts and producers. But he was very much on his way.

Fields cites the rule-book to Bud Jamison in "The Dentist."

The Mack Sennett Shorts

Mack Sennett and Bill Fields were kindred spirits and good friends. Mack had been a fan of Fields' since his Ziegfeld Follies days, and therefore undoubtedly the only real obstacles to an immediate merger had been Sennett's tight-fisted attitude toward a dollar, and Fields' generous estimation of his own monetary worth. It was inevitable, however, that the two golfing companions who so frequently discussed comedy and grandiose script possibilities as they strolled across the links would eventually get together.

Just how the chemical fusion was worked will probably never be known. If Robert Lewis Taylor's account is full of historic holes, doubtless they were dug by Sennett himself, and Sennett's own version, in his autobiography, *King of Comedy*, is a fabrication of fantasy without even the courage of its own unconviction. Sennett's book, a jumble of flashbacks and jumps in time, constructed somewhat in the manner of "Citizen Kane," is almost always hazy about dates and facts (although a most readable volume, and probably a reliable guide as to his modus operandi). Sennett suggests quite definitely that Fields was working for him in the twenties, and describes in minute detail a fruitless attempt to stage a whale-chase comedy with Fields.

The comedian, a notoriously bad sailor at the best of times, afraid even of the short crossing between the California mainland and Catalina Island, was below-decks the whole time: either sea-sick, imbibing liquor in an effort to build stamina or, more likely, both.

Sennett writes that he was then paying five thousand dollars a week to Fields and had to write the whole sea venture off as a loss, rushing a "golfing" comedy into production right away in order to get something of Fields on film. (Fields didn't develop his golf routine until later, and the only golfing bit that he and Sennett ever worked on together took up only a small percentage of the footage of their 1932 two-reeler, "The Dentist.")

Sennett also refers to Harry Langdon as one of his newest stars, and accuses the arbitrary Fields of turning down his comedy ideas with a "Great for Langdon —but not for me." This then would seem to set the date as 1924, Langdon's first year with Sennett. But spinning his yarn still further, Sennett laments that while Fields was turning out profitable comedies for him, his own thoughts were on making another Mabel Normand feature comedy, and that he had developed a script called "The Extra Girl." Since "The Extra Girl" was made in mid-1923, that sets the alleged date of the Sennett-Fields liaison back by another year or more.

In passing, it is worth noting that in his book Sennett takes Mabel Normand to task for her impossible and unreasonable salary demands of three thousand dollars a week for that picture, demands which seem most reasonable indeed. She was, after all, a big star and "The Extra Girl" was to be a big picture, and she would have had to be generous to the point of lunacy to have accepted two thousand a week less than Sennett was paying the new and relatively unknown Fields for appearing in shorts.

It would be nice to think that Sennett was right, and that hidden away in a dusty San Fernando Valley vault awaiting rediscovery are a dozen or more priceless W. C. Fields two-reelers made in the early twenties. But alas! the facts indicate otherwise. Nevertheless, the legend of the early Fields-Sennett association goes marching on (perhaps helped on its way by Fields' own boast in "The Bank Dick" that he used to be a director for Sennett), and has now been repeated so many times that it is firmly entrenched in American movie mythology, a worthy running-mate of the Holy Grail and the Loch Ness Monster.

The only authenticated association between Sennett and Fields took place late in 1932. The king of slapstick had never regained his footing after the advent of sound. Even his last silents, made without top stars or directors, had been below his highest standards. He maintained a prolific output of two-reelers and even made one or two mediocre features during the first five years of sound, but his farces were largely unfunny and labored, and the combination of obvious verbal jokes, complicated plotting and old-fashioned looking, badly done slapstick was an uneasy one. The films were acceptable then because Sennett's name still meant something and there was a relative dearth of slapstick two-reelers, but few of them hold up today.

Only in the handful of comedies that he made with really strong personalities—Fields, Bing Crosby, and to a lesser degree singer Donald Novis—did he achieve any real success. Since Sennett was releasing through Paramount it seems more than likely that the studio itself suggested his employment of Fields (already under contract to Paramount) so that Fields could re-establish his film popularity in comedy shorts while the front office pondered what kind of vehicle might be best suited to him.

Paramount was notorious for its Procrustean tendency to take unique personalities and, rather than tailor stories to fit them, re-shape the personalities until they resembled conventional stars and fitted existing properties. Thus the career of one of their most promising stars of the twenties, Betty Bronson, was sabotaged when the studio brains faltered before the task of finding more whimsy and magic to follow up her superb Barrie films, "Peter Pan" and "A Kiss for Cinderella," and tried instead to turn her into a second-string Clara Bow or Colleen Moore. Fields' Sennett shorts may have been made at precisely the right time to prevent a similar fate from befalling him.

The first of these to appear was "The Dentist." Fields wrote the story himself under his own name. His penchant for such imaginative nom-de-plumes as Otis Criblecoblis, Mahatma Kane Jeeves and Charles Bogle came later. His director was Leslie Pearce, a competent run-of-the-mill film-maker but no more. However, Fields' films were seldom hurt by bad directors or helped by good ones; ability to get along with the Great Man and avoid friction always was the key requisite of a Fields director.

"The Dentist" also had Babe Kane as his back-talking daughter, Bud Jamison as a golfing companion, and, most notable, the lanky and languid Elise Cavanna as a much-put-upon patient. Miss Cavanna was to Fields what Margaret Dumont was to Groucho Marx, and whether she played patient or wife she made a magnificent foil for him in three of his Sennetts.

"The Dentist" begins with a fairly placid breakfast, but hostilities break out when daughter Babe Kane, bending over the ice-box, mistakes Fields' gentle tap for a caress from the ice-man. "What do you have against ice-men?" she pouts, "Red Grange was an ice-man." "He's still an ice-man!" Fields retorts. When the ice-man arrives to deliver a huge block of ice, Fields promptly chucks him out and announces that he will take care of the ice—which turns out to be much too big for the ice-box.

Fortunately, the phone rings. Fields deposits the ice on a lighted gas stove and answers the phone. It is his pal, reminding him of their golfing date. Hanging up, Fields picks up the now considerably smaller block of ice and tosses it into the ice-box.

"Did you manage the ice?" his daughter calls from the other room. "It was easy," Fields mumbles distractedly, now preoccupied with gathering his golf-clubs, which are determined not to cooperate. On the golf links things do not go so well. Fields loses the ball after a drive, and his search for it is fruitless.

After watching him scour the links, a sweet little old lady who just happens to be there confides that if it won't spoil his fun she can tell him where the ball is. "It's under that leaf," she points out. Fields' snarled and furious "Thank *you!*"—he doesn't say "you old bag," but you can hear it anyway—fortunately escapes her. Anxious to be on with the game he yells "Fore!" and drives —this time his ball knocking another player senseless. Fields waits with growing impatience, and then insists that the body be dragged away so that he can play through.

His caddy (Bobby Dunn) is of course a constant irritation; it is his presence, the way he looks, or breathes, or stands, that Fields considers at fault for the failure of his drives, and he delivers a merciless tongue-lashing to the caddy. "The kid's so dumb he doesn't know what time it is," complains Fields. "By the way, what time is it?" asks his companion. Fields doesn't know.

Taking advantage of the rule book, which says that under certain conditions the ball may be dropped by hand, Fields studies distance, angle of turf, wind velocity—and drops his ball so that it rolls gently into the next hole. His pal is aghast, but Fields will brook no argument against his record-breaking hole-in-one. But his triumph lasts only until they reach a water trap. Two balls are lost in it, and in the Fields temper tantrum that ensues, the clubs follow the balls.

"Oh, you can't do that," complains his buddy, dismayed at such poor sportsmanship. But Fields not only can but does, and the hapless caddy follows balls and clubs.

At his office after the game, Fields is in a better frame of mind. His first patient is a fellow golfer, and Fields is delighted at a chance to regale him with the story of his hole-in-one. Seeing an element of unspoken doubt on his friend's face, Fields is on the verge of losing his temper again. "What do you mean, I can't do that . . ." he begins, citing chapter and verse from the rule book.

A woman patient (Elise Cavanna), screaming in pain, arrives in the outer office, but Fields ignores her as he launches into a story about an inept medical competitor down the street: "He treated a man for yellow jaundice for eleven years, and then found out he was a Jap!" Another patient is ushered in, a pretty young woman with attractive legs who says she has recently been bitten by a dog. To demonstrate, she bends double, pointing to the scar on her ankle where she was bitten.

Fields, viewing the spectacle from behind, jollies her along with "It's fortunate it wasn't a Newfoundland dog!" Finally he gets her seated in the dental chair and asks if she'd like gas. "Well, gas or electric light—I'd feel nervous having you fool around me in the dark." Without wasting time over such niceties as an anesthetic, Fields gets right to work with his drill—and at the end of the lengthy procedure, the squirming woman's hand, quite by accident, is in his pocket.

Giving her a look that expresses his hatred and distrust of all womankind, he dismisses her and gets down to the more serious business of practicing aiming

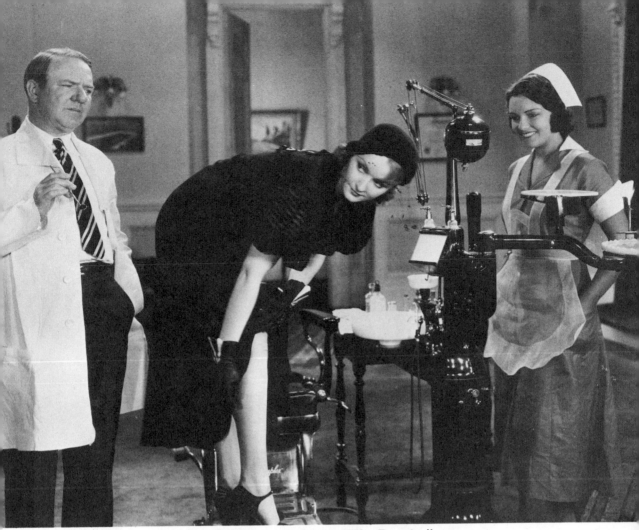

"It's fortunate it wasn't a Newfoundland dog!"; "The Dentist."

with his duck-hunting gun. The screams of the woman patient in the outer office are becoming more agonized. "Tell her I'm out," he instructs his nurse, letting fly at an imaginary duck. But the woman, unable to bear her suffering any further, has marched in of her own accord and heard this last remark. She is outraged, but Fields covers the situation with some rumbled pleasantries.

As he adjusts the dental chair for her, he turns to his nurse and berates her, *sotto voce*, for being remiss. "If I say I'm out when these palookas show up, then I'm out. . . . Don't let these buzzards come in here whenever they feel like it!"

Beaming kindly at his patient, he makes final adjustments to the chair, which then rises majestically toward the ceiling and falls down again with a thump. "Just come in for the ride?" he asks pleasantly. A cursory examination of the patient's mouth soon shows him what is wrong. "Just hand me that 404 circular buzz-saw," he tells the nurse, and with the vicious-sounding instrument going full blast in the unfortunate lady's mouth, he accompanies his work with that peculiar, tuneless and lyric-less song, "Grubbing!" (the title is also the sum total of the words, which are repeated endlessly), a song that Fields was fond of war-

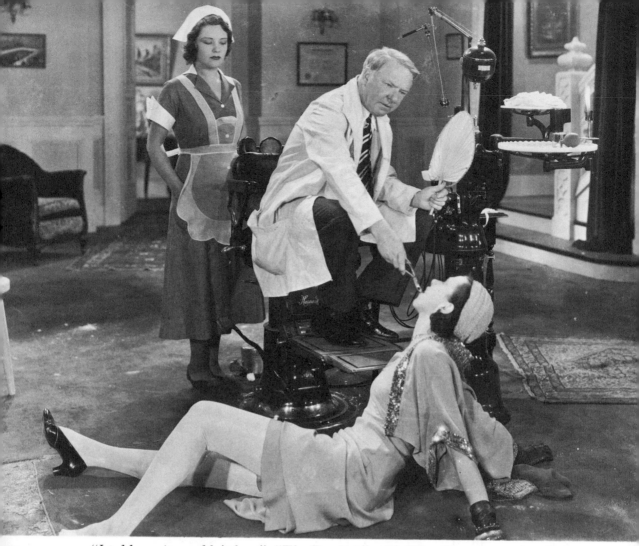

"I told you it wouldn't hurt"; "The Dentist," with Elise Cavanna as the victim.

bling while engaged in such professional activities as dentistry, barbering or store-keeping.

At the end of the ordeal, and as his patient is composing her tortured body after the contortions the treatment has put her through, Fields smiles the mirthless professional smile of all dentists, and says, "There you are; it didn't hurt a bit, did it?"

Family matters distract him for a moment, and he takes leave of his patient to go and lock his daughter in her room. She has been threatening to run away with the ice-man. No amateur at temper tantrums herself, she proceeds to jump up and down on the floor. In Fields' office below, the chandelier sways perilously and ominous cracks appear in the ceiling. A huge chunk of plaster falls with a thunk into the patient's wide-open mouth. Fields dives in with his forceps to retrieve it, and the battered patient, in a moment of dazed optimism, remarks, "Why, it came out easily, didn't it?"

Fields rushes upstairs again, battering on the door, demanding to be let in, until his daughter reminds him that he has the key. Like any parent reluctantly forced to administer discipline to an unruly offspring, Fields grabs his daughter —and twists her arm painfully. Locking her in again, he returns once more to his office. The ill-used Elise Cavanna has now left, and in her place enters a curious little man in the most theatrical of makeup—patently phoney black hair-piece and sideburns and a long black beard. Fields applies himself to the task of inspecting his new patient's teeth. First he has to find the man's mouth, and exploratory forays into that dense beard produce no results.

"Say 'Ah'," instructs Dr. Fields, and using a stethoscope, he gradually traces the source of the sound. Triumphantly he pushes back the black foliage to reveal the mouth: "And a very pretty thing too!" he compliments his patient in his most unctuous manner. Without waiting for any information as to the patient's problem, he plunges in with his drill, standing back a moment or two later to allow the bearded one to spit a shower of teeth into the basin. At that moment a honking bird wings by, and Fields grabs his rifle to shoot a fusillade at the ceiling. The possible fate of his daughter upstairs is not elaborated on, and the film finishes in an explosion of gunpowder and falling plaster.

The least unified of his four Sennett shorts (the others concentrated on one specific routine instead of, as here, a group), "The Dentist" was also one of the very few Fields vehicles to show him in a wholly unsympathetic light. The cheating, the lack of consideration, the outright cruelty shown by Fields in this film were unmatched in any other, nor was there even a token attempt to justify his behavior. This made it hardly less funny—and it is often uproarious—but Fields must have known that "The Dentist" presented a serious flaw for a comedy image that was intended to endure, and in his remaining shorts for Sennett, Fields did much to show a warmer personality, without lessening the bite of his humor.

"The Fatal Glass of Beer," which was released some three months later, was almost universally disliked at the time. Exhibitors complained that it had no story and no slapstick; audiences were puzzled, constantly waiting for it to "take off" and go somewhere, which it never did. All it had was Fields, which in those days was hardly enough. Even confirmed Fields fanciers felt let down by it. Actually it was another case of a brilliant little film being offered at the wrong time, before the public was attuned to such bizarre and even black comedy.

The film also suffered from a total disregard of the rudiments of production value, let alone polish. Back projection, or the "process shot," a valuable economy, was murderously exploited. In a scene, Fields is standing in front of a motion picture screen on to which is projected ancient stock footage of a reindeer herd, and he literally dares even the most unknowing of laymen not to see the trickery. The reckless lack of finesse—and this extends to substandard sound quality—has a value all its own and is entirely appropriate to the rough-and-ready tale that Fields is spinning, a kind of burlesque of Robert W. Service's rugged poems about Alaska.

Fields' director this time was Clyde Bruckman, a first-rate comedy man but one whose milieu was the more visual films of Keaton and Lloyd, where he was able to make use of his other talents as a writer and gag-man.

Fields again wrote the story, if it could be so described, and it has no perceptible line as such. A running gag, repeated at regular intervals, has Fields, swathed in the furs of a Northern trapper, going to the door of his cabin, looking out benignly at the stillness of the great outdoors, and intoning "And it ain't a fit night out for man nor beast," whereupon an offscreen stagehand belts him in the face with a handful of very artificial-looking snow.

"The Fatal Glass of Beer" opens with Mr. Snavely (Fields) sitting in his storm-besieged cabin and being disturbed by a knock at the door. "Who's thar?" he asks in the phoney he-man tone he uses throughout the short. Out of the howling blizzard, a Mountie (Dick Cramer) enters, knocking several layers of snow and ice from his furs.

"Stopped snowing yet?" Fields asks conversationally.

The two rugged outdoor men swap tales for a few moments, then Fields announces with studied casualness, "I figured on goin' over the Rim tonight!"—evidently a considerable undertaking.

The Mountie, a sentimental soul, gets to talking about Chester—Fields' son, who came to a bad end in the big city—and asks Fields if, before he leaves, he would sing once more the song he wrote to commemorate the sad fate of Chester. Fields is happy to oblige, and sits down with his zither, first making sure that etiquette is observed by inquiring, "You won't consider me rude if I play with my mittens on?" The song that follows is a tuneless, rhymeless and almost endless saga of the misadventures that befell Chester in the wicked city, and the fatal first glass of beer that inevitably led him to smoking, bad company, wild women, and eventual imprisonment for theft.

This tale is unfolded with occasional cutaways to Chester (George Chandler) in the big city. These scenes are staged and acted in an exaggerated burlesque of Victorian melodrama, and every time he reaches a particularly telling line in his musical narrative, Fields pauses to smile understandingly and a trifle wistfully at his Mountie audience, who is now in tears. The descent of Field's wastrel son reaches the depths of depravity when Chester, in the throes of delirium tremens, is approached by a Salvation Army lass collecting for charity—"and wickedly he broke her tambourine," before she responds "with a kick she learned before she had been saved."

The final lines of the incoherent but hypnotizing ballad point the stern moral lesson that anyone who goes around breaking tambourines is bound to end up in the hoosegow.

As the Mountie wipes away his tears, Fields delivers a final word of wisdom: "As my Uncle Ichabod once said, the city ain't no place for women, gal, but pretty men go thar . . . he was always saying something to make you split your sides laughing!"

Babe Kane receives parental chastisement from Fields in "The Dentist."

It now is time for Fields to leave his little line cabin and head for home over the Rim. He mushes his dog-team (one of them a dachshund) through the snowy wastes, taking time out to comment that the unconvincing-looking snow tastes like cornflakes. At his home cabin, he greets some Indians who are sheltering there with a condescending "Hello thar," and then ejects them into the blizzard.

There is some byplay with two electric lights, which work only when the cord for the opposite light is pulled. Then, with wife Rosemary Theby (a worn, tired-looking woman, frequently type-cast in earlier years as a downtrodden hillbilly wife), he sits down to one of the most unappetizing of all movie meals. It consists primarily of a huge, unattractive communal bowl of soup and a three-foot-long loaf of bread, something like a baseball bat, which Fields breaks in two, carefully measuring one piece against the other to make sure that he gets the bigger one.

His wife tells him that another creditor is on his trail again and is about to seize his dog team. "He won't take my lead-dog," Fields gargles through a mouth-

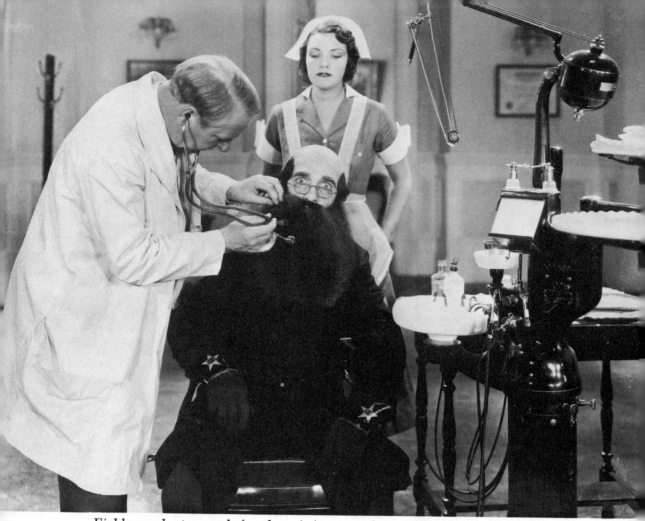

Fields conducts search for the missing mouth in "The Dentist."

ful of bread and soup, looking smug, " 'cause I ate him. He was mighty good with mustard."

There is a knock at the door. It is Chester, home from prison. Fields rushes to greet him, in his haste planting one foot in a wooden bucket, clattering across the floor wearing it like an outsize clog. The reunion is tearful, snow from Fields' bowed head falling into the soup to join its other unspeakable ingredients. Overcome with emotion, Chester says that he has come home to stay, and what he wants to do first is to crawl into his own little bed and sleep like a baby.

"Why not lie down and get some rest first?" Fields suggests helpfully.

The good-nights turn into a three-way barrage of endearments and advice on how to get a good night's sleep. "Good-night, son, and don't forget to open your window. . . ." "I won't, ma, and don't forget to open your window . . . good-night, pa, and you open your window too, pa. . . ." The triangular conversation, with everyone speaking at once, reaches a crescendo and is brought to a halt only by the slamming of Chester's door.

Fields loved to mock the time and energy wasted on meaningless socializing and everyday small talk, and this little vignette was one of the simplest and funniest episodes he ever devised along those lines.

Chester safely in bed, Fields decides, "I think I'll go out and milk the elk." In shaky, faded and wholly unconvincing back-projected shots, the reindeer herd gallops past Fields, who calls in vain for his pet reindeer, Lena. As one of the stock-shot reindeers pauses, seemingly to stare at him, Fields stares back and asks, "Elmer, have you seen Lena?"

Thwarted, Fields gives up the idea of elk's—or reindeer's—milk and settles for water instead, although the old wooden pump disgorges only blocks of ice.

In Chester's bedroom, the woebegone Rosemary Theby is confronting her remorseful son, and she draws from him the confession that he did indeed steal the bonds for whose theft he was sent to prison. She is not surprised, but makes him promise not to tell his father, for the devoted man has always believed in his boy's innocence, and the truth would break his poor old heart.

Moments after Miss Theby has left, Fields enters the room on a like mission. He is understanding and sympathetic, and he draws the same pitiful confession from his son, forgiving him for his sins, but urging him to keep the truth from his mother. Chester, to prove his thorough reformation, goes on to tell how he took the "tainted money I got from them bonds, and threw it in the river," and came back home, cleansed and repentant.

"To sponge off us for the rest of your life," growls the now less paternally inclined Fields—and with the help of his wife, who has been listening at the keyhole, he grabs the night-shirted Chester and heaves him out into the snowy wastes.

Mr. and Mrs. Snavely stand arm in arm by the open door, staring at the great off-screen wilderness. "And it ain't a fit night out for man nor beast!" Fields intones for the last time, raising his fist to ward off the expected deluge of snow which this time, to his consternation, does not materialize.

Fields' last two Sennett comedies, "The Pharmacist" and "The Barber Shop," both had a little more production value and better film style, perhaps because Arthur Ripley directed them. A decidedly off-beat craftsman who made relatively few films, Ripley had started off as a writer for Sennett in the twenties, and drifted later, in the forties, into such semi-surrealistic thrillers as "The Chase" and "Voice in the Wind." Like Gregory La Cava, his performances were erratic, but he was a gifted and disciplined film-maker, and one who was able to bring in completely non-assembly-line films on strictly assembly-line budgets. He would seem to have been a particularly apt director for Fields, and it is unfortunate that their collaboration did not extend to some of the later features.

"The Pharmacist" presents Fields as an unusually (for him) good-natured store-keeper, reasonably happy in his home life, at least tolerated by a wife who is less of a shrew than usual, and with two daughters—one at the romantic age, the other a gawky brat of ten—as the only real bones of contention in his life.

Mealtime in "The Fatal Glass of Beer"; gold nugget Fields has just discovered can be seen beside Rosemary Theby's elbow.

Returning from an errand, Fields shoos some playing children away from the front of his store. Inside, two old-timers who have been playing checkers since early morning are still pondering over the next move. Fields studies the board, knowingly warns against several moves, and finally nods his silent approval. Of course, the unfortunate recipient of his advice makes the move and is cleaned out in one fell swoop.

Fields' wife calls him to lunch, and he immediately becomes embroiled in an argument with Babe Kane, his recalcitrant younger daughter. Bursting into tears, she bawls "You don't love me any more!" Fields takes a swing at her, assuring her, "Certainly I love you!" His wife tries to mollify him, but his feelings are still hurt. "She can't tell *me* I don't love her!" he growls.

This particular household, unlike most of Fields' later homes, is not averse to alcohol, and pre-lunch cocktails are shaken on Babe's pogo-stick. However, when Babe's behavior at table includes mixing up the cocktail olives with chewing gum, she is forbidden further lunch. She manages to satisfy her hunger pangs by stealing the canary's bird seed and then (mercifully off-screen) eating the canary

"Do you have a female attendant?" Fields and customers; "The Pharmacist."

itself. Fields, aghast, removes the parrot to a position of greater security, while Babe coughs up a shower of canary feathers. Meanwhile, his older daughter carries on an endless telephone conversation with boy-friend Cuthbert.

The phone rings down in the store, and Fields rushes down, hoping it will be a sale. It is. "A box of cough-drops. . . . The two men with the whiskers? . . . Yes, we have them . . . no, we couldn't split a box. . . . Yes, we deliver . . . eighteen miles on route thirty-six, and then another four miles on route two. . . . Yes, we'll send out our truck this afternoon."

Two ladies enter the store, obviously embarrassed by their delicate and feminine mission, and ask if there is a female attendant. Graciously Fields tells them that his wife will be down in half a tick. His wife is less than enthusiastic, however; she will have to change, and this gives her a chance to complain that she hasn't any decent clothes to wear. Anxious not to lose the sale, Fields rushes down again to assure the ladies that his wife will be right with them, and launches into a chorus or two of "Grubbing."

Fortunately, a male customer arrives to divert him. A belligerent-looking man, he is unsure of what he wants, and as he meanders slowly down the counter inspecting the various wares, Fields moves along with him, cheerfully and smilingly trying to interest him in some of the specialties of the house without resorting to high-pressure salesmanship. He points out some of the exciting literature that can be purchased: "*Mother India? The Sex Life of the Polyp? The Rover Boys?*"

The customer is obviously not a reader, so Fields tries another approach: "Cake à la mode?" Another curt turndown. Fields jiggles a little doll on a string —"Amusing little beggar!"—and holds up an indeterminate novelty item which he describes as "Old Moscow in Winter." No sale. Finally an inspiration: how about a postage stamp? "Yeah," agrees the surly customer. "Gimme a stamp. One of the purple ones."

Unfortunately there are no purple ones in stock, although Fields obligingly offers to paint one. But the customer is now more concerned with delivering a tirade against the tyranny of a democratic government that tells you what color stamps to use. At length he agrees to buy a three-cent stamp, purple or not, and Fields starts to tear one off. "No, not one of those dirty stamps," insists the customer. "Give me a clean one!" Patiently Fields removes a stamp from the very middle of the sheet—even though it means using scissors and destroying several stamps immediately surrounding it.

"Shall we send it?" he asks.

The customer is willing to carry it provided it is wrapped and placed in a large paper bag. Unfortunately he doesn't have the three cents in cash, and offers a hundred-dollar bill. Fields, of course, can't change it, and suggests that the gentleman pay next time. As the customer is leaving with his package, Fields suddenly calls him back, recalling that they are giving away a free souvenir with each purchase that day. From under the counter he produces an enormous vase which the customer accepts somewhat grudgingly and departs.

The two ladies are becoming rather impatient waiting for the arrival of Fields' wife.

Preening herself, she comes down the stairs with a welcoming smile, and without waiting for Fields to get out of earshot, the younger of the women asks if there is a ladies' room that her mother can use. Somewhat less charmingly, Mrs. Fields points to the rest room, and goes back upstairs in a huff.

Another customer, an officious looking one, comes in and whispers a request into Fields' ear. Suspicious, Fields takes a fan down from the shelf, plugs it in, and watches as the breeze blows open the man's coat, revealing his detective's badge.

"Certainly not!" booms the outraged Fields. "I have never sold alcohol here, and would never cater to such depraved tastes."

The two ladies reappear, mother whispering a request that daughter is too embarrassed to pass along. But finally daughter is persuaded; could her mother please have one of those wonderful souvenirs? Not only mother but daughter too is presented with one of the magnificent vases, and they leave happily, promising to come back if they ever need to buy a stamp.

Suddenly the serenity of the store is blasted by machine-gun fire as cops outside do battle with an escaping gunman. Amid the chaos, the phone rings with a complaint that the cough-drops have not arrived yet. "I can't understand that," Fields lies ingratiatingly. "The truck went out an hour ago."

Rushing into the store, the crook menaces everybody with his gun and is knocked cold by a man who has been using the phone. A woman who has fainted from the excitement is brought in. "Get her a drink, give her some brandy!" the bystanders urge, while Fields—the detective at his elbow—is hard-pressed to explain why he cannot be a good samaritan. Someone causes the unconscious crook's gun to go off, and the frightened Fields' arms shoot up, knocking off his topless hat, which descends neatly over the arm of the prostrate woman.

Cops remove the crook, and, the excitement over, Fields thanks the young chap who knocked out the crook and introduces him to his older daughter as the man who saved his life. "Cuthbert!" she shrieks, astonished to find that the two-reel phone conversation has been conducted from her father's store. Cuthbert is played by that genial oaf Grady Sutton, who was to play Fields' prospective son-in-law in "The Bank Dick," too. This time Fields is quite satisfied with his daughter's choice and the film ends on a note of satisfaction all around—for all but the customer who is waiting for his cough-drops.

"The Barber Shop" repeated the general pattern of "The Pharmacist," even to the climactic set-to with an escaping crook. But the aura of domestic well-being had definitely taken a turn for the worse. Fields' wife not only detests and browbeats him, but also insists on serving a strict vegetarian diet, even though a good steak is (or has been) one of the joys of Fields' life.

Fields plays Cornelius O'Hare, barber, and we first see him sitting on the sunny sidewalk outside his parlor, stropping his razor and testing it on the tip of his tongue. As the townspeople pass by he greets them cheerfully, agreeing with the current points of view of each, then telling the audience what he really thinks of them once they're out of earshot. He shoos a little dog away from his barber pole: "Get away, think all I've got to do is paint that pole all day?"

His son is given to complex riddles, delivered usually at the dinner table, and Fields does his inadequate best to answer such gems as, "Why is a long journey like a cat's tail?" Despite much fancy verbiage, he is unable to come up with the correct answer—"Because it's fur to the end!" Sensing his wife's disapproval, he urges son Ronald, "Eat your spinach, eat your spinach!" yet defends Ronald's riddle-making talents. "Mr. Lincoln used to be very fond of telling riddles, and that, as much as anything else, made him the fine President that he was."

His wretched meal over, Fields goes down to his barbering parlor again. A customer has brought in a huge bass fiddle, and leaves it there for the day, propped up against Lena, Fields' own bass fiddle. The manicurist, Hortense, returns from an enjoyable steak lunch, and to take his mind off his stomach, Fields plays her a new composition on his fiddle.

As he paddles and thumps away, explaining the intricacies of his finger movements, he says wistfully, "Funny, my wife doesn't think it's music." An old customer comes in for a shave, but Fields isn't sure that he recognizes his face. "No, it's all healed up since the last time I was in here!" is the explanation.

The new shave gets under way, but Fields' attention is diverted by a pair of pretty legs on the sidewalk outside, and his customer seems momentarily in danger of losing his nose.

"Is that a mole on your chin?" Fields asks pleasantly. "Yep, had it all my life." The razor swishes murderously. "You don't have it any more!"

A customer who is enormously fat enters and declares that he must lose weight or his wife will leave him. Fields laughs mirthlessly and directs him to the steam room, locking him in securely after first pointing to all the warning devices he can sound if things get too hot. The steam room is operated by a fire engine in the back yard. "Get hot, Ethel!" Fields instructs the engine as he sets his machinery in motion.

Back with the customer in his chair again, he becomes disconcerted by the presence of a patiently waiting and begging dog, and explains that last week he accidentally cut a man's ear off. The dog got it, and ever since. . . . "Get away, get away!" he shouts to the dog, diplomatically cutting the story off before its pay-off.

The shave completed, the barber adds the *coup-de-grâce* with the hot towels. They are too hot to be touched with naked hands, and Fields picks them up gingerly with a pair of tongs, dumping them on his customer's face and assuring him, "It's all right, I've got them!" as he piles the loose ends of the towels atop the customer's shrouded head, now enveloped in hissing steam. Leaving his client to relax for a moment he wanders outside to greet Mrs. Broadbottom, who is walking her baby. The infant is playing with a jumbo-size safety pin, which Fields removes with the admonition that swallowing it could kill him. His kindness is repaid by the baby with a solid clout to the head with a full milk-bottle, and Fields promptly returns the baby's naked safety pin.

Frenzied hootings and honkings from the steam room call him inside again. The steam room door is blisteringly hot, and he can open it only by wrapping cold towels around the handle. From the inferno emerges the formerly fat man, now a midget swearing law suits and revenge. But Mrs. O'Hare is calling, and that takes precedence.

"Yes, my slender reed?" Fields answers. She is going shopping for clothes and needs money. "Got change for a dollar?" he asks her generously, but she snatches the money out of his hands and stalks off. An Amazonian mother comes in with a little girl who needs a haircut but doesn't want one. "Oh, come on, have your hair cut," Fields pleads and wheedles. She has just been to a party and is

Fields, a robber and an unwilling patron; "The Barber Shop."

wearing a trick hat; as he removes it, another is revealed underneath. Fields decides to cut her hair with her hat on, and moves on to weightier matters, such as the current newspaper accounts of an escaped bank robber. Telling the admiring manicurist, Hortense, of the days when he was a member of the Bare-Handed Wolf-Chokers Association, he wishes he could spare the time to go after this robber himself.

On cue, the robber appears and commands the barber to get rid of his other customers pronto and shave off his moustache and sideburns. In vain Fields tries to direct him to the much better barber down the street, and weakly explains to the Amazonian mother that this gentleman was there ahead of her. Terror-stricken, he races out of the shop, leaving Hortense to her fate. Grabbing a bicycle, he rides madly down the town sidewalks, bellowing at some chickens out for a stroll, "Get out of the way, you fools!" It is a small town, and in a matter of minutes he has circled it, arriving back at his shop just as the robber has decided it is time to leave.

Son Ronald, across the street, bats a baseball which hits the robber and knocks him into Fields, and the two of them tumble into his parlor together.

Oblivious of pedestrians, Fields makes a getaway from the bandit in the climactic sequence of "The Barber Shop."

Hortense is visibly impressed by her employer's prowess; Fields, not knowing that his adversary is unconscious, seeks to apologize. "Some of my best friends are bandits . . . the president of the bank comes up to my house!" Then, realizing the situation, he turns it to his advantage and starts posing as the modest hero to his incredulous wife and the townspeople who crowd in.

An observant cop causes his little world to crumble instantly, however. He brings in Ronald and tells the assemblage, "Here's the brave little man who caught the robber. He knocked poor Mr. O'Hare off his bicycle . . . are you hurt, Mr. O'Hare?"

"Not physically, no," groans Fields as his disillusioned fans depart. But Hortense still believes in him. "No use arguing with those people," he explains, "they're all excited!"

Suddenly there is a curious noise from the corner of his shop, and he goes to investigate. His bass fiddle and the customer's are slumped together, and as he straightens them up, a litter of baby bass fiddles is revealed. "Lena!" he exclaims in shock and outrage, kicking the offending male fiddle to shreds before throwing its tattered remains out into the street.

As a postscript to his four Sennett shorts, Fields also appeared in a minor Warner Brothers one-reeler of 1933 entitled "Hip Action," directed by George Marshall, number three in a series of Bobby Jones golfing shorts that went by the overall title of "How To Break Ninety." Warner Brothers had adopted the fairly familiar practice of the day in using big names to enliven and give more general interest to what would otherwise have been a routine sports reel. Comic Fields, villain Warner Oland and character player William B. Davidson helped and hindered Bobby Jones, and by their simulated ineptitude helped spotlight his own expertise.

Shorts were turned out in prodigious numbers by all the major companies in the early thirties, and had to be made quickly and economically. The big names who appeared in them had to be cooperatively willing to accept less than top-grade material and to work at top speed. Fields' adaptability to those two requirements has never been remarkable, so it is not surprising that this would turn out to be his only guest stint in a short of this nature.

Fields as the stony-hearted villain of "The Drunkard," the play-within-a-play climax of "The Old-Fashioned Way." (Courtesy of Paramount Pictures)

☞ 10.

Too Much Footage-
Too Little Fields

No fewer than eight W. C. Fields films were issued in 1933 and 1934. He breezed through all of them in fine style, but the perfect Fields vehicle was a long time in being developed, and in half of those films he was kept off-screen for dangerously long periods by a studio that was still uncertain of how best to use him. In the first of this group, "International House," Fields was allowed only fleeting moments in the first two-thirds, but he took command in the final third so completely—and so recognizably to the film's benefit—that it is hard to understand why doubts about Fields' staying power were not dispelled immediately. As an entity, "International House" has the disjointed, off-the-cuff look of "Million Dollar Legs," probably because of a last-minute decision to transform a serviceable comedy script into a partial musical extravaganza.

Thanks largely to Busby Berkeley, Ruby Keeler and Dick Powell, the big musicals were on their way back as potent box-office attractions. "International House" gathers together an assortment of comedy and musical names, many of them appearing only in specialty numbers seen on the revolutionary new televi-

Fields, preparing for the night; with Peggy Hopkins Joyce; "International House."
(Courtesy of Paramount Pictures)

sion set, then still termed a "radioscope," which motivates the flimsy plot. Rudy
Vallee, who was in for a song; Colonel Stoopnagle and Budd, popular then but now
antiquated and unfunny, and Cab Calloway and his orchestra are among the show
business personalities introduced through the TV device. Calloway's contribution, a
lively number called "Reefer Man"—a paean of praise to the joys of marijuana
smoking—implies that all Negroes and jazz musicians function only when "flying"
on reefers, and latter-day television editors must have been grateful indeed that
Paramount simplified their work by presenting the number only as a TV specialty,
without intercuts to essential plot or characters.

For all of its slapped-together look, "International House" is a handsome
film, with luxurious sets, some ingenious special effects, and an elaborate slapstick
finale that must have been expensive to prepare and stage. The one big production
number, though probably inspired by Busby Berkeley, is at pains not to imitate
his unique style. The girls, sparsely dressed in cellophane and transparent silks, and
in costumes representing coffee-pots, cups and saucers, are both pretty and exotic,
and the extremely mobile camera, swinging overhead or gliding along the floor

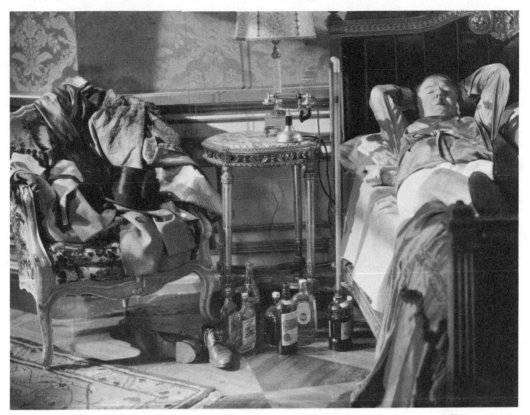

Fields as a gentleman of leisure; "International House." (Courtesy of Paramount Pictures)

through archways of perfectly matched legs, makes the most of them.

The plot, such as it is, concerns a television machine thrown open to international bidding by a Chinese inventor. Bela Lugosi plays the Russian representative with mock dignity, Stuart Erwin is the rather dim-witted American who wins out in the end, and Burns and Allen are the hotel's doctor and nurse respectively. Considering the mechanical quality of their long and overly measured exchanges of gags, their material wears surprisingly well and is still funny. Franklin Pangborn is very much in his element as the harried and prissy hotel manager, and Peggy Hopkins Joyce—convincingly if self-consciously playing herself, with none-too-subtle gags poking fun at her marital notoriety—very unfairly is accorded top billing above Fields.

As Professor Quaill, Fields has literally only a few seconds' footage in the first half of the film, clambering into his plane, "The Spirit of Brooklyn," and loading it with enough liquor to sustain him on his journey. Occasional radio reports comment on his progress and on the number of victims laid low by empty bottles dropped from his plane. Flying over pagodas and the other Oriental architecture of Wu Hu, site of the television demonstration, he lands his plane in the hotel grounds and bawls out, "Is this Kansas City, Kansas, or Kansas City, Missouri?"

"Wu Hu!" calls back the irked Franklin Pangborn. Fields sizes him up with an expression of some distaste, and removes the flower from his own lapel. "Don't let the pansy fool you," he replies somewhat icily. Fields then joins the guests, spins a rambling yarn about how he lost his way (attributed mainly to his having removed the needle of the compass to darn his socks) and is soon juggling with a candle. "Will you join me in a glass of wine?" asks Miss Joyce graciously.

"You get in first, and if there's room enough, I'll join you," was Fields' reply.

The locale of "International House" gives Fields ample scope to indulge in jokes about Orientals—whom he always found both endearing and amusing—and to wear a variety of kimonos. These fascinated him too, to the extent of his insisting that one of his steady girl-friends wear one at all times.

One of the running gags after Fields' arrival is the periodic disruption of the reception desk, with Fields testing out the pens and squirting ink on the manager's shirt front; riding roughshod over swarms of guests demanding prior attention; becoming embroiled in all the telephone lines from the switchboard ("A Chinese noodle swamp!" he roars as he blithely disconnects all the callers); and finally knocking over the huge mail rack, so that all of the carefully filed letters and room keys are deposited in one vast heap at Franklin Pangborn's feet. This gag is repeated with three or four frenetic variations until it reaches its pre-ordained climax. Anticipating another onslaught, Pangborn, in a fit of delirium, wreaks the havoc himself.

The shortage of rooms compels Fields to seek his own accommodation, and not unexpectedly he winds up in Peggy Hopkins Joyce's bedroom, the two just missing each other as they wash, undress (closeups of the Joyce legs cutting to closeups of the less attractive Fieldsian underpinnings) and hop into bed from opposite sides. Jealous ex-husband Bela Lugosi is a witness, and goes gunning for Fields. The sequence is less funny than it might be, although it is a useful build-up to the eventual climax when the Fields-Lugosi showdown erupts into a tour-de-force slapstick chase.

Ejected from the Joyce boudoir, Fields finally settles for a less romantic sleeping partner in the person of the Chinese inventor, who still hasn't fulfilled his heart's desire—to get the Six Day Bicycle Races at Madison Square Garden on his radioscope. Retiring for the night, the Chinese tells Fields, "I always sleep on my stomach," to which Fields offers the not-at-all illogical comment, "Don't you find it gets all wrinkled?"

Breakfast the next morning is mainly a matter of hard liquor, but since he is in the Orient, Fields adds a touch of elegance to his room-service order: "Bring me up a bird's nest and a couple of hundred-year-old eggs boiled in perfume."

The television demonstration is a success, even though Fields detests Rudy Vallee and talks back nastily to his TV image, which in turn talks back to Fields.

With Gracie Allen, in "International House." (Courtesy of Paramount Pictures)

Newsreel footage of battleships letting loose with their big guns seems to irritate him even more. He takes a shot at them with his revolver, and the hapless battleship leading the parade promptly sinks beneath the waves.

Ambling down a corridor seeking his room again, he opens a door—to be greeted by a female scream which indicates that it is not his room. Mumbling a cheerful apology, he moves on to the next room. This time he's more careful, and peeks through the keyhole first. Again it is not his room, but apparently the sight is quite interesting. "What won't they think of next?" he mutters incredulously.

Miss Joyce, who has taken a "genuine" romantic interest in Fields now that she has heard he is a millionaire, is planning a getaway with him when the vengeful Lugosi arrives on the scene with his cronies. Fields has been demonstrating his midget car to Miss Joyce, and also some gags that went back to "Sally of the Sawdust," including his head sticking out through the roof of the car and the problems of placing a top hat squarely over it. In the course of all this, Miss Joyce's skirt has somehow been ripped off, and Lugosi is in no mood for explanations.

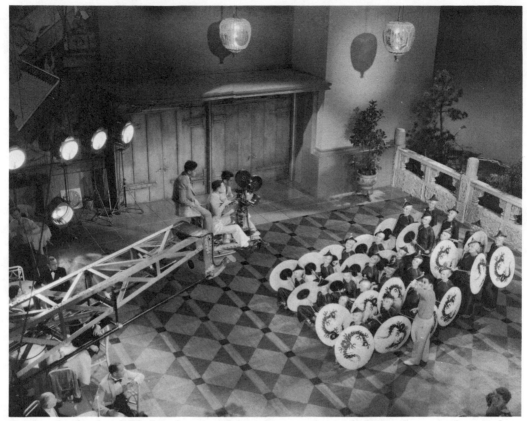

Eddie Sutherland, behind two camera operators, directing musical number;
"International House." (Courtesy of Paramount Pictures)

A marvelous slapstick chase ensues, with the midget car careening all over
the hotel, through the lobby, up in the elevator, down a fire escape (the matching
up of model scenes with full-scale action is extremely skilfully done), upstairs,
and finally onto the roof where the car trundles directly into Fields' plane. As
they rise into the air and safety, Miss Joyce discovers that she is sitting on something. She rises to reveal a litter of nondescript kittens. "I wonder what their
parents were?" she asks of Fields, giving him the straight-line for the climactic gag
of the film as he replies, "Careless, my little cup-cake, careless."

"International House" re-united Fields with his old director friend Eddie
Sutherland for the first time since "Tillie's Punctured Romance," and augured well
for their future collaborations. Alas, however, that collaboration was not maintained on Fields' next picture, "Tillie and Gus," the one picture above all others
where he really needed a director, for this was the first of his talkie features to be
constructed as a Fields vehicle. For once, he was there all the way through, and
despite the able collaboration of Alison Skipworth and Baby Leroy, he had to
carry the film almost alone.

"Tillie and Gus" was given to a new director, Francis Martin, as a kind of trial. Martin, who had been one of the writers on "International House," had played in silent short comedies, and written and directed quite a few of them, as well as writing a number of sound shorts. But he had never written a solo screenplay, nor had he directed a feature. "Tillie and Gus," which he wrote in collaboration with Walter DeLeon from an original story by Rupert Hughes, was his first feature as a director, and his last. He was promptly returned to collaborating with others on screenplays, including several subsequent Fields films, and for the next ten years never strayed from his own particular fold again.

"Tillie and Gus" is amusing and entertaining, but entirely too gentle and subdued. The potentially rich material is mined on the surface only, and while it is peppered with superb one-liners from Fields, good sight gags, and some colorful supporting characters—especially Clarence Wilson as Phineas Pratt, one of the most hissable of all grasping lawyers—it all has the look of being a dry-run for something that will be very funny when they do it with all the stops out.

The best sequences appear at the beginning of the film, when Augustus Winterbottom (Fields) and Tillie Winterbottom (Skipworth), believed by their family to be dedicated missionaries, are shown in their true surroundings. Tillie is running a saloon-bordello in China, and Gus is a card-sharp about to be run out of Alaska, after a trial in which he pleads eloquently but ineffectually on his own behalf. Both Winterbottoms return to America to claim an inheritance and accidentally meet on a train, where they collaborate to fleece some suckers in a card game. All of this is fine stuff and promises well for the rest of the picture. But when they reach their destination, the film seems unable to settle on a point of view.

They discover that the legacy is small, and in any case has gone to a young couple (Clifford Jones and Jacqueline Wells) with an infant son (Baby LeRoy). The confidence couple scheme against the crooked lawyer on his own level, while maintaining their pose as missionaries for the benefit of the young couple who admire them so innocently. With Fields undergoing a gradual reformation, his tiltings with Baby LeRoy are subdued; and since so much time has been agreeably employed in establishing the Fields and Skipworth characters, relatively little time remains in the short (fifty-eight-minute) picture for anything more than brief development and wrapping-up of story-line.

The Fields-Clarence Wilson plotting and counter-plotting afford some enjoyable moments, and there is some genuinely funny slapstick involved in the reconditioning of an ancient ferry boat which offers the youngsters their only chance of paying off their debts. The film comes to a fairly rousing conclusion with a race between two ferry boats for a government franchise, the battered hulk captained by Fields winning hands down (by decidedly unfair means) over the streamlined new luxury boat entered by the villains.

This climactic steamboat material draws some of its gags from Buster Keaton's "Steamboat Bill, Jr." (Fields throwing a life-preserver overboard, whereupon it sinks beneath the waters immediately), and was itself to be of some influence on the later and superior steamboat race done by John Ford as the climax to Will Rogers' "Steamboat Round the Bend." Baby LeRoy is left on deck in a bathtub which eventually slides off into the river, and is doomed to sink the instant his exploring fingers pull out the plug. Realistically staged, this episode is a little too suspenseful to be as funny as Fields' frantic efforts to rescue him should make it. The rescue pulled off just as the tub plummets to the bottom of the river, Fields, who by now has completely mellowed toward Baby LeRoy, turns his sadistic sense of humor on Clarence Wilson, whom he also—but very reluctantly—saves from drowning.

"Tillie and Gus" has the aura of a much-later Fields, as though made when he was still in fine fettle but when his pictures began to lack bite because of the "wholesome" restrictions clamped on by the Motion Picture Production Code. It is hard to place this consistently amusing but punches-pulled comedy in the brittle, free-wheeling year of 1933. Nevertheless, although a missed opportunity —and seemingly a confirmation to Paramount that they had reason to ponder the effectiveness of Fields in a showcase vehicle—"Tillie and Gus" is not without charm, and if anyone were ever so audacious as to try to list all of the Fields films in order of merit, it would probably be closer to the top than to the bottom.

Although, like all of the other Paramount stars appearing in it in guest roles, he had very little footage, Fields quite walked away with his next film, "Alice in Wonderland." For some inexplicable reason, the film gives director and production designer William Cameron Menzies a screenplay credit along with Joseph L. Mankiewicz. However, it is quite evident that he worked on the physical design of the film, and was probably an assistant to director Norman McLeod, a maker of slick romantic comedy who seemed a curious choice indeed for this film.

Lewis Carroll's bizarre work has always defeated Hollywood, the whimsy and magic of "Alice" escaping the streamlined cuteness of Disney as surely as it eludes McLeod and Menzies here. Doggedly faithful to the text of Carroll, and with a genuine nightmare quality untempered by balancing qualities of charm, it is a clumsy work, and one is too often distracted by the game of spotting the various stars (Gary Cooper, Cary Grant, Richard Arlen and many others) behind their totally impenetrable disguises. But Fields, as Humpty Dumpty, seems to fit physically and mentally into Lewis Carroll's world as logically as he would later fit into Dickens' world in "David Copperfield." His Humpty Dumpty façade seems like a logical extension of his true self, and the absurd yet somehow logical lines of Lewis Carroll could almost have been written for Fields' delivery. Only he, Mae Marsh (as the Sheep) and Charlotte Henry (a thoroughly charming Alice, if somewhat less tiresome than the one Carroll gave us) managed to retain their own identities in this rather grim charade, where the odd moments of horror (the living Christmas Puddings, waiting to be eaten) worked extremely well, but where the essential whimsy was too heavy-handed and swamped in décor to be effective.

"Six of a Kind," Fields' next film, gave him the expert comedy craftsman Leo McCarey as a director—the same McCarey who had made some of the most charming Charlie Chase situation comedies and some of the wildest Laurel and Hardy slapstickers, who had worked with both the Marx Brothers and Eddie Cantor and would later specialize in the sophisticated romantic comedies with Cary Grant. Not that the director—good or bad—would have made much difference to Fields' portions of "Six of a Kind." He came in late in the film, delivered a pool-room routine that was solely of his own conception and execution, and required no more of a director than insuring that there was film in the camera and that the set was lighted up.

The title was very much of a misnomer, for at least two of the six were decidedly *not* of a kind. The plot had Charlie Ruggles and Mary Boland deciding to celebrate their second honeymoon by motoring cross-country to Hollywood, taking along George Burns, Gracie Allen and their Great Dane to help share expenses. Ruggles and Boland played beautifully together as they always did, underplaying the obvious, injecting underlying warmth into scenes of straight comic bickering. But even allowing for the fact that Burns and Allen were supposed to be nuisances, their obtrusive and unfunny dialogue patter (far less effective here than in their pithy, undisguised vaudeville interludes in "International House") brought the film to a grinding halt far too often in the first two-thirds of the film.

When the party reaches Nevada they encounter Sheriff Hoxley (Fields) and his friend, saloon-keeper Mrs. Rumford (Skipworth). The Skipworth collaboration is only nominal this time. Fields proceeds to usurp the screen for his own ends, taking up a pool game with warped cues, but never actually getting around to hitting the first ball because his attention is constantly wandering to the labyrinthine tale he is unfolding of how he came to be called Honest John.

The story, like the game of pool, is never really consummated, but at least one gathers from it that the Honest John appellation had its beginnings in the fact that Fields once returned an acquaintance's glass eye when it happened to bounce out of its socket.

There is some climactic hue and cry involving thieves and detectives, and Fields runs around the hotel in his night-shirt muttering his familiar curse about the Ethiopian in the fuel supply, but after that classic game of non-pool, nothing else really matters. He has wrapped the whole film up neatly, having stolen it—not without some opposition—from Ruggles and Boland, and yanked it out contemptuously from under the feet of Burns and Allen.

That no print should be available today of "You're Telling Me," Fields' fifth film in his 1933-34 group, is—in terms of motion picture history at least—a major disaster. It is one of far too many films that exist today only in a kind of limbo because of a maze of tangled rights and copyright problems. A re-make of Fields' silent "So's Your Old Man," it was originally based on a *Redbook* story by Julian Street, and Paramount's motion picture rights expired many years ago. Were Paramount to decide to reissue the film or re-make the property once more it would presumably be simple to negotiate a renewal of those rights, but in the meantime ownership of the film, or such ownership as is possible to verify, has passed along

W. C. Fields, aboard steamboat; "Tillie and Gus." (Courtesy of Paramount Pictures)

to Music Corporation of America together with all the other post-1929 Paramount pictures acquired by MCA for television distribution.

For a different company to re-negotiate rights is a more complicated procedure than for the original producing company to do so, and MCA—faced with this problem on a number of properties—invariably considers such complications not worth the effort involved, especially since the handful of films concerned hardly affect the marketability of their huge blocks of films. So pictures such as Fields' "You're Telling Me" and Lubitsch's "Bluebeard's Eighth Wife" become consigned to a celluloid no-man's-land and eventually are doomed to extinction, since if nobody actually owns them, nobody is likely to spend money on their preservation.

The tragedy of "You're Telling Me" is that it was the first Fields sound vehicle, other than the disappointing "Tillie and Gus," to do him justice and to establish the basic formula for the handful of classics to come. Although one's personal memories of the film can be enthusiastic and are backed by extremely complimentary contemporary reviews, which not only praised the film for its comic

Fields, with Alison Skipworth, in "Tillie and Gus." (Courtesy of Paramount Pictures)

invention but stressed the warmth and Dickensian quality that Fields brought to his role, such a landmark film has to be made available for reappraisal before a reliable opinion can be formed. Certainly it was a notable progression from the original "So's Your Old Man," making only superficial changes in details (the shatterproof glass invented by Fields in the first version becomes puncture-proof rubber tires in this one) and benefiting from the addition of J. P. McEvoy dialogue. As his director, Fields had Erle C. Kenton, who was sufficiently versatile to have made some of the best and most silken pseudo-Lubitsch comedies of the twenties and some of the grimmest horror films of the thirties and forties.

As an example of the way Fields constantly polished and improved upon his gags, one can cite the instance of his attempted suicide—a "black" sequence that he managed to make hilariously funny, just as Chaplin managed to make the planned (and abandoned) murder of the street girl in "Monsieur Verdoux" both warm and touching.

In the original silent, Fields' suicide attempt is foiled when the bottle of poison he is about to swallow is accidentally smashed. Then he chances to meet a princess traveling incognito and, seeing her with a bottle of iodine before her, imagines that she too intends suicide and devotes himself to changing her mind. In the re-make, Fields' inventive skill prevents his taking his own life—he pours iodine into a collapsible spoon of his own design, which immediately folds up under the strain. But when he encounters the princess—about to apply iodine to a cut—sound permits him to lecture her on the moral wrongs of suicide.

Since "You're Telling Me" also included the celebrated golf game in its tight sixty-six minutes of pure Fields, it was a most rewarding experience for the legions of Fields followers who had waited so long to see him in a worthy screen vehicle. The only moviegoers who had any cause for complaint were the fans of Larry "Buster" Crabbe, the swimming champion, who had been introduced as a handsome new athletic hero only the year before in "King of the Jungle," and who was wasted here in a straight leading-man role. It was to be but one of a series of mediocre leading-man, villain and even minor supporting roles for Crabbe, who, like Fields, had serious career problems at Paramount, although, *un*like Fields, he had started out with the perfect star vehicle and then spent the next five years in time-wasting nothings.

Released in late 1934, "Mrs. Wiggs of the Cabbage Patch" (the third of four movie versions of the time-honored old tear-jerker) was the last Paramount film that exploited Fields for his name and gave him almost nothing to do. He was listed second in the cast, Pauline Lord as Mrs. Wiggs preceding him, and since there were no other big names in the picture it was logical that exhibitors should give him preferred billing in all their advertising. Yet his appearance in the eight-reel film was restricted to the last reel and a half, and because the sentimentalities of Mrs. Wiggs were exactly the qualities to appeal least to Fields fanciers, audience patience tended to wear a little thin through the hour or so preceding his introduction. Moreover, the Fields name attached to such a title automatically implied (though as it happens, erroneously) that a beloved classic of rather slurpy Americana had been reshaped and possibly even burlesqued to accommodate the comedy star; thus many of Mrs. Wiggs' most fervent boosters stayed away from her first reincarnation on the sound screen.

"Mrs. Wiggs of the Cabbage Patch" (like "Seventh Heaven") works far better in the silent version, not because it is old-fashioned (although in a literary sense it is) but because it romanticizes poverty in a way that is acceptable in the purely visual, only semi-realistic world created by the silents. Sound and dialogue remove the invisible barrier that makes the silent world of imagination plausible, and they bring us into contact with a tangible world where we are up against reality, where motives and solutions must be explained through the harsh logic of speech and cannot be circumvented by a convenient and poetic subtitle.

Nevertheless, the 1934 "Mrs. Wiggs of the Cabbage Patch" had charm, warmth, a realistic evocation of small-town Americana in the horse-and-buggy era, and a particularly well-done sequence of a visit to see a troupe of traveling players at the town's opera house. Pauline Lord managed to avoid an excess of

Fields the mariner; "Tillie and Gus." (Courtesy of Paramount Pictures)

syrup as Mrs. Wiggs, and the film as a whole was better done than Henry King's sound re-makes of those two other and kindred silent classics, "Way Down East" and "Seventh Heaven." (The latter was the ideal example of a love story working superbly as a silent, and failing dismally because of the added dimension of sound.)

No little credit for the comparative success of "Mrs. Wiggs of the Cabbage Patch" must be apportioned to Norman Taurog, always a good director with children and emotional subjects. If "Mrs. Wiggs" didn't quite recapture the poignancy of his earlier "Skippy," it was a worthy try.

Fields stumbles into the film in reel seven as Mr. Stubbins, the mail-order husband of neighbor ZaSu Pitts. No sooner is he on screen than he has a run-in with a little urchin, and entangles himself in the complicated mechanics of opening a gate. Not only is his entrance long overdue, but comedy has been conspicuously lacking in the recital of the Wiggs family's cheerful struggle against poverty, culminating in the death of the frailest Wiggs son.

Audiences greet Fields' entrance with far greater laughter than anything he

With Tammany Young; "Six of a Kind." (Courtesy of Paramount Pictures)

Fields and co-conspirators Bob McKenzie and extra; "You're Telling Me." (Courtesy of Paramount Pictures)

Fields indulges an Oriental predilection in "International House." (Courtesy of Paramount Pictures)

actually is doing at that point justifies, but it is a sincere greeting to an old friend and an indication of hope that matters have taken a turn for the better—not just for Mrs. Wiggs, but for the audience too. But in the subsequent climactic reels little is done to make the most of Fields' presence, possibly out of respect to the original material and to a determination that Fields should remain subservient to it.

As the husband-to-be, he is something of a gourmet, and insists only that his wife be a first-rate cook—which she is not. Mrs. Wiggs, a culinary wizard on a non-existent budget, chips in to cook the critical dinner, and Fields, delighted with a monumental feed, capitulates happily to matrimony—and presumably to years of anti-climactic meals. The delectable Fields small-talk and flowery compliments to the bedazzled ZaSu Pitts are a joy, but the film offers him little else. When the "End" title flashes on so soon after his initial appearance, and without his having played pool, juggled or had his watch dipped in molasses, there is inevitably a sigh of audience disappointment. Fortunately, however, Paramount was about to make spectacular atonement. His *magnum opus* and the finest film of his career, "It's a Gift," was due for release within a few weeks.

As the villain of "The Drunkard," with Judith Allen; in "The Old-Fashioned Way." (Courtesy of Paramount Pictures)

Fields Hits His Stride

Although it was to be but a prelude to two even finer comedies, "The Old-Fashioned Way," released in late 1934, was far and away Fields' best talkie to date. Its flamboyant mood was established by presenting the titles and credits as if they were old circus posters, and its plot got under way in the very first scene, in which a lawman is seeking the whereabouts of The Great McGonigle. A trite romantic sub-plot involving Fields' daughter with the stage-struck scion of a socially prominent family did not interfere substantially with the story, and it seems churlish to criticize a film for old-hat dramatics when the film itself bears such a disarming title.

Fields wrote the original story himself, using the pen-name of Charles Bogle, a character name he had lifted from "You're Telling Me." The film marked his only collaboration with William Beaudine, a first-rate director whose later prolific specialization in formula "B" pictures (notably the "Bowery Boys" series) tended to obscure his long earlier career as a productive director in the realm of comedy. He made some of Mary Pickford's best silents, and his several English-made films included "Windbag, the Sailor," one of the best films of Will Hay.

"The Old-Fashioned Way" once again presents Fields as the small-time theatrical impresario, forever one step ahead of the law. This time his little turn-of-the-century group of traveling thespians is offering a production of that barn-storming old melodrama, "The Drunkard." The final third of the film is devoted to a presentation of that play, with many of the original cast members repeating their own roles and Fields having the time of his life playing the villainous Squire Cribbs.

As the picture opens, the sheriff is at the railway depot to prevent McGonigle's troupe from leaving town. Forewarned, Fields sneaks up behind the sheriff, sets fire to the legal writ clasped in his hands, and meanwhile, with perfect timing, engages the sheriff in conversation. "I have something for you!" announces the sheriff, producing with a flourish the blazing writ. "Thanks!" Fields beams, lights his cigar, and swings aboard the train just as the writ crumbles into ashes.

On the train there is some minor problem over tickets, but Fields turns the conductor over to "my assistant, Marmaduke Gump." While the conductor is busy counting heads, another passenger has the misfortune to drop his sleeping-berth ticket close to Fields' foot, beneath which it immediately disappears.

While the hapless and now bedless passenger argues with the conductor, Fields' daughter, played by Judith Allen, asks her father what is under his foot. His air of innocence doesn't fool her any more than does his story that he bought the ticket for her just that morning. Fumbling in his pockets, protesting that he most certainly had a sleeping-berth ticket for her, he finally agrees that just possibly this ticket might have been dropped by the passenger who was standing in that exact spot, and since of course he has no wish to be dishonest, he will return it to him.

Warning his daughter that he may play a little parchesi before retiring, he hurries to the sleeping car and quickly settles into his stolen berth—first pushing the still protesting passenger out of the way, and indignantly complaining that his noisy argument with the conductor is lowering the tone of the train to that of a cattle car.

After a comfortable night in his stolen berth, he descends the next morning by stepping on the ample stomach of a large Turkish gentleman in the berth below. The man's broken-English protestations annoy Fields, who remarks, "What are you, Chinese peoples?" Later, when the man returns from the washroom, Fields hits him a resounding clip on the head with a croquet mallet borrowed from a little boy. Boy and father retrieve the mallet from Fields, father waving it belligerently as the giant Turk emerges once more from his berth just in time to jump to the obvious conclusion.

While father is being throttled, Fields beats a tactical retreat to the washroom, where the unfortunate who involuntarily gave up his berth to Fields is huddled uncomfortably on a bench. Pushing the man out of the way, that he may attend to his ablutions more easily, Fields proceeds to denude the towel stand of its contents, using one towel to wipe his face, another for his hands, and a third to cough in.

Fields, with sunflower and slight misapprehension; "The Old-Fashioned Way."
(Courtesy of Paramount Pictures)

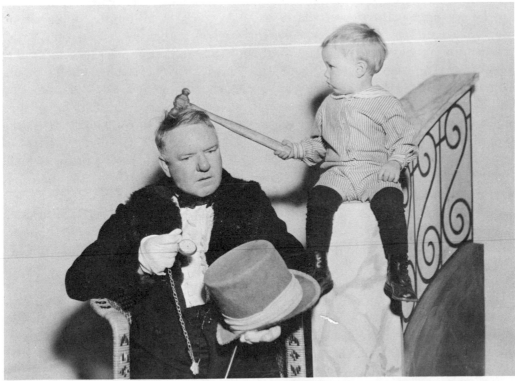

Under assault by arch-enemy Baby LeRoy, in "The Old-Fashioned Way." (Courtesy
of Paramount Pictures)

The whole sequence of sleeping berth and washroom contained gags and bits of characterization that were to become perennials with Fields, and indeed the entire sequence was reconstructed—the locale having been changed to an airplane—in his much later "Never Give a Sucker an Even Break."

As the train approaches their destination, the sleepy little town of Bellefontaine, Fields dons his most impressive regalia, consisting of tall hat, an outsized sunflower for his buttonhole, and a magnificent overcoat that seems to balloon out toward its base like a pyramid. Seeking to bolster the morale of his underfed and long unpaid troupe, he reads them a fabricated telegram from his agent. Since the telegram addresses Fields as "the world's greatest tragedian," his thespians do not put too much stock in its message that the next engagement is sold out in advance. As Fields comes to the end of the long and unlikely telegram, he stares defiantly at the camera as he reads the signature of the telegram—a signature one can safely assume had not appeared in the original script. With teeth clenched, he hisses out the name of his agent—one Snead Urn! And he adds, "I wouldn't be surprised if they had a brass band to meet us."

Remarkably, there is a band. Accompanied by the town dignitaries in fine uniforms, the band has come to honor an official of a brotherhood lodge—that same official who lost his bed to Fields the night before—who now tries vainly to make his presence known from behind The Great McGonigle, who is graciously acknowledging the tributes of the crowd and expressing his humble appreciation for this recognition of his artistry. As Fields rambles to the end of his florid speech, in which he has dealt with the sad lot of those whose destiny it is to wander the world over, knowing only fame, adulation and wealth, he reaches out his hand in greeting. But at last the real guest of honor has made his escape from the train, and Fields is ignored. The departing lodge-brethren hoist their swords on high, and one of them neatly spears Fields' hat just as it is about to settle on his head.

As in most of the towns he visits, McGonigle has his sucker-list prepared well in advance; this time he and his troupe will stay at the boarding house of Mrs. Wendelschaffer, on whom they have imposed in the past. The gate to her neat little garden is wide open, but even so Fields has trouble getting through it; twice his cane catches in the wicker-work, stopping him short and toppling his hat in the dust. The acting troupe gets safely ensconced in Mrs. Wendelschaffer's abode just in time to take part in a mad stampede for lunch.

Seeking to establish his prestige right away, Fields addresses the assembled guests in a grand manner, outlining his many accomplishments "for the benefit of all those who don't know me," while he fastidiously crumbles crackers in his white-gloved hands. One of the guests happens to be Cleopatra Pepperday, an aging and thwarted singer (Jan Duggan) who has the added talent of being very rich. As he enters, Fields observes that she is "dressed like a well-kept grave," but recalls that on his previous visit to Bellefontaine she was more than a little enamored of him. In order to impress her with his charm and good nature, he even steels himself to suffer with fortitude the indignities heaped upon him by her little son Albert, played by the diminutive and gurgling Baby LeRoy.

Though reacting with embarrassment and horror when the infant affectionately greets him as "Dada," Fields retains his *savoir-faire* even when the little fellow dunks his watch in the molasses, where it sinks like a rock in quicksand. Retrieving the sticky timepiece with a peeved, "The minute hand won't be a bit of use," he reassures the baby's clucking mother that he is not in the least annoyed.

"How can you possibly hurt a watch by dipping it in molasses?" he purrs. "It just makes me love the little nipper all the more!" LeRoy's aggressive behavior continues, however, accompanied by deprecating smiles from his mother, who makes no attempts to curb her offspring but merely remarks "I don't know *why* he's behaving like this; you should see him when he's alone."

"Yes," replies Fields with a barely suppressed snarl, "I'd like to catch him when he's alone!" But when Baby LeRoy overplays his hand by splattering Fields with potato salad, his temper nears the breaking point. "Brat!" he thunders, then spells out the word for the benefit of the little tyke.

The meal finishes, and the diners depart. LeRoy is left alone with Fields, and the danger of his position is clear even to him. His face takes on an innocent air, and he crawls on all fours out of the room, helped by Fields, who—making sure that nobody is looking—delivers a hearty kick to the youngster's backside!

McGonigle's first move in Bellefontaine is to woo the willing Cleopatra, promising her a big part in his show—even hinting at matrimony—in return for her financial backing. Cleopatra sings him an endless and repetitive ditty. After complimenting her on her genius, Fields turns on his romantic charm. The spontaneity of his wooing is somewhat hindered by Cleo's artificial curls, which come loose under his caressing hand and which he furtively tries to pin back in place while he continues with his tender endearments. Enraptured, Cleo promises to place her future—and her finances—in Fields' hands.

The landlady enters, and Fields, anticipating a distasteful inquiry about the rent, thrusts one of Cleo's discarded curls under his nose as a moustache, assumes a German accent, and claims not to understand English. The deception falls apart when the bogus moustache falls into Fields' hat just before he puts it on. He stalks out of the room somewhat inelegantly, one foot having embedded itself in a basket of knitting, and Cleo's curl swinging from the back of his head like a pigtail.*

This whole element of Fields' wooing of Cleo and the delightful counterplaying of Jan Duggan, good-naturedly taking a rather cruelly written role in stride, is one of the highlights of the film, beautifully paced and timed.

---

* Seemingly spontaneous bits of business like this were anything but, nor were they merely the result of years of experience and polishing. Each such sequence, regardless of how many variations on it Fields had performed earlier, was mathematically choreographed for its usage in a specific situation. Fields' original scripts, now in the possession of the Gene Fowler family, are covered with his own hand-written marginal notations, outlining in infinite detail every gesture, grimace and hesitation to be employed.

The production of the play-within-a-play, "The Drunkard," works on two levels—firstly, as that rare thing, a burlesque of something that is already a burlesque and that still manages to seem fresh and amusing. And secondly it continues to be hilarious on its own plot level as the somewhat sketchy story-threads are drawn together. Hero and heroine are finally united. The show itself is almost brought to a halt by Sheriff Prettywilly, who has another of those legal documents which were forever being waved under Fields' nose and which Fields disposes of here with a tolerant smile and the explanation, "Evidently intended for *Ichabod McGonigle!*"

Poor Cleopatra's starring role is whittled down to one line of dialog which seems to bear no relation to anything or anyone in the show, and while she spends the entire evening in the wings practicing variations on that one key line, she never does get to speak it! On stage, Fields falls victim to sundry theatrical disasters, being knocked off into the orchestra pit, having the curtain fall heavily on his foot—and rise again, only to take his wig with it. But he hams it up magnificently as the villainous squire, complete with top hat, black curly hair, and a crooked witch's cane. The whole roaring melodrama is played purely for laughs, yet while never pulling its comedy punches, it leaves enough of the old drama intact to indicate a certain respect for it.

Frequent cutaways to the enthralled and excited audience also pay a kind of tribute to the built-in head of steam that the old play once had. An intermission affords the leading-man, Joe Morrison (a pleasing singer of rather short-lived fame in the thirties), to sing a traditional old "mother" ballad entitled, "A Little Bit of Heaven Known as Mother." Cutaways to a mother and son in the audience, tearfully embracing, play the sentiment for laughs, yet this whole sequence has such a genuine nostalgic feeling for the theatre and its audiences of that period that burlesque remains just that, and never becomes cruel parody or ridicule.

Needless to say, a good deal of this version of "The Drunkard" is pure Fields, including his standing by an open door, intoning, "And it ain't a fit night out for man nor beast!" to the anticipated fistful of prop snow. The performance concluded, Fields has no wish to let either his theatrical or his movie audience go home as yet, so he promptly brings on his entire juggling act, including a routine involving the manipulation of large boxes which seem to fall through space in a kind of slow motion so that they are exactly where Fields wants them at just the right time.

This was the only occasion when Fields didn't have to sneak his juggling into films as a cutaway or a wrap-up; it is a full vaudeville act, performed in a close shot and without camera or editing tricks to enhance Fields' dexterity. No such tricks are necessary, and Fields, obviously proud and pleased at the chance to record the act on film, is at his best. When the lengthy (but for enthralled audiences, all too short) act is climaxed by a tomato hurled at Fields by Baby LeRoy, audiences invariably burst into spontaneous applause.

The wooing of ZaSu Pitts; "Mrs. Wiggs of the Cabbage Patch." (Courtesy of Paramount Pictures)

This climax of "The Old-Fashioned Way" is one of mild pathos, the kind of climax that "Sally of the Sawdust" had worked toward and then avoided. In order to see his daughter happily married and away from the atmosphere of hustling that will always be his, Fields pretends to desert her so that he can accept a lucrative offer as a solo performer. In actuality, he is descending even lower in his professional scale by becoming a medicine show impresario, but since this is the kind of life he loves, it is hardly a bitter-sweet ending in the tradition of Chaplin's "The Circus."

In any event, Fields leaves his audience with a solid laugh rather than a wistful tear. Trying to sneak his luggage out of the boarding house without paying, he is caught in the act by the vigilant Mrs. Wendelschaffer, who demands to know what he is doing. Cunningly, he adopts a wheedling tone and spins a tale about a down-on-his-luck friend whom he has invited to share his quarters. The landlady of course won't hear of yet another free-loader entering her home, and demands that Fields return the luggage to the street.

"Oh, very well," he mutters, "but you'll regret this in the morning!"

With helper (Tammany Young) and the bad-tempered Mr. Muckle (Charles Sellon); "It's a Gift." (Courtesy of Paramount Pictures)

"It's a Gift," Fields' last 1934 release, not only was his best comedy, but surely must also rank among the finest comedy work from any period and any country, in its own way the equal of René Clair's "The Italian Straw Hat," Buster Keaton's "The General," Laurel and Hardy's "Big Business," Harry Langdon's "Tramp Tramp Tramp," and the best work of directors Ernst Lubitsch and Preston Sturges.

In this, his best film, Fields creates a complete reversal of the image that time, the critics, and he himself have stamped out for him; he plays a humble, good-natured fellow, quite lacking in opportunism and even the milder forms of cruelty, though not above occasionally slipping one over on his obnoxious son. Completely downtrodden by his family, he doesn't even allow himself the "worm finally turns" scene that was so satisfying in "The Man on the Flying Trapeze," and when he wins through to riches and a happy ending without any real effort, for once the audience feels that he has earned his reward if for no other reason than his having been a good fellow all his life.

Based partly on elements of his silent films "The Potters" and "It's The

Old Army Game" (both written by J. P. McEvoy), and partly on his own material, "It's a Gift" is a rich and warm comedy with a great deal of shrewd and acidly accurate observation along the way. Basically it is divided into four key comedy sequences linked by a slim overall plot in which Fields, dissatisfied with the humdrum life of a grocer, sells out over the opposition of his family and moves to California, where he has bought an orange grove. Although the film's tour-de-force episode—the hilarious "sleeping porch" sequence, which takes almost two reels of footage—occurs at the midway point, the whole film is so skilfully constructed that the story itself gathers momentum thereafter, and the later comedy sequences are themselves faster and more devoted to physical action, so that there is at no time a sense of anti-climax.

The opening sequence establishes Harold Bissonette (Fields) as far from the master in his own household. His oft-expressed wish to move to California is constantly pooh-poohed. His selfish daughter fears that she will be separated from her boy-friend, and Mrs. Bissonette—the superbly domineering Kathleen Howard—is convinced that the gamble will lose what little security they already have. Although Fields is first to the bathroom every morning, he never yet has managed to complete his shaving in peace. Daughter Mildred, constantly opening and closing the medicine cabinet, monopolizes the mirror, while her short jabs with powder and lipstick are a menace to Fields' shaving arm. Finally he is forced to suspend another mirror from the lamp cord, and to shave himself from a squat and uncomfortable position as he follows the mirror in its circular peregrinations.

Daughter finishes her beauty treatment and abandons the wash-stand and mirror just as Mrs. Bissonette enters and throws up her hands at the insane spectacle her husband presents. "Why don't you use the mirror?" she asks logically and with a long-suffering sigh that indicates that this kind of behavior is fairly commonplace.

On his way down to breakfast Fields steps on an abandoned roller skate at the top of the stairs and descends rather more spectacularly than he had intended. The conversation over breakfast centers around a distant relative who is expected momentarily to die. Mrs. Bissonette pays lip service to his many virtues, but admits that she could put the inheritance to good use. Junior Bissonette is frankly delighted at the prospect of the death in the family and, indeed, can hardly wait.

A living has still to be earned, and Fields sets off to open his little grocery store which he runs with the inept assistance of one of his most frequently used stooges, Tammany Young. Business is brisk this morning. Jasper Fitchmueller, one of the town's most pompous citizens, wants a pound of kumquats, and he wants them in a hurry. A lady asks, "What do you have in the way of steaks?" "Nothing in the way of them, we can get right at them!" responds Fields pleasantly, donning a fur coat before entering the freezer to bring out the meat.

Engaging in a hectic conversation on the side with his assistant concerning the kumquats—Mr. Fitchmueller is fast losing his patience—Fields rests his elbow on the scales accidentally, calculates the weight and cost of the steak and wraps it in tissue paper. The lady customer, no doubt used to these eccentricities, accepts the overcharge and far-from-dainty packaging as among the fortunes of war. While the search goes on for the kumquats, Fields tactfully suggests possible substitutes, but Fitchmueller is adamant. But all other trade is forgotten when Fields spots Mr. Muckle, the blind man, heading for his store.

Using the afflicted for comedy purposes in film has rarely been inoffensive. I can think of only one joke in which the afflicted are made the butt of the gag and which is still funny in its own right; this occurs in Buster Keaton's silent "The Playhouse." Two one-armed men sit side by side in a vaudeville theatre. When the acts are over, each applauds by clapping the other's hand. The system works well until they disagree on the merits of one particular act; one of the men is delighted, the other one less enthusiastic. Declining to applaud himself, he sits on his one hand so that his partner can't applaud either. For the most part, though, gag men were careful to construct gags around the blind, the deaf, the dumb, the lame or the misshapen in such a way that the joke rebounded onto the lead comedian. A notable example is found in one of the better Sennett shorts of the twenties, "Skylarking," in which the hero, proudly showing off his new automobile, has to stand by in horror while the tapping cane of a blind man systematically breaks windows, windshield and lights, a combination of pity and embarrassment preventing him from intervening.

Fields' handling of the blind-man sequences in "It's a Gift" is masterly, not least because the blind man is also a little deaf and more than a little crotchety. Charles Sellon, a valuable sour-puss in many films of the thirties, plays Mr. Muckle. Fields can't quite get to the front door in time to open it for Mr. Muckle. "Hah! Had that door closed again!" grunts Muckle as his wildly waving cane plows its way through the door's plate glass.

Apologizing for the inconvenience, Fields sets Mr. Muckle down and returns to Mr. Fitchmueller, the agitated kumquat customer. But Mr. Muckle's wandering cane is exploring again. "Hold it, honey . . . *please*, Mr. Muckle!" entreats Fields. But Muckle's cane has already wreaked its havoc. "Don't worry," Fields assures him, "nothing serious. Just the new consignment of light bulbs!" Muckle persists in making his way to the counter, and decides that he wants a stick of chewing gum, which Fields wraps and hands to him.

"You don't think I'm going to lug that all over town, do you?" snaps Muckle. "Send it!" On the way out, he successfully demolishes the other plate glass window with a cheerfully chiding "Ah, you had that door closed again!" and then plods slowly across the normally sleepy main street, which is now alive with fast traffic and clanging fire-engines, all of which miraculously miss him.

Mrs. Dunk (Josephine Whittell) and Baby Dunk (Baby LeRoy, of course) are out for their morning promenade, and Mrs. Dunk and Mrs. Bissonette exchange small talk about the coming inheritance. Mrs. Dunk, smoothly catty, recommends a new dress shop which does wonders for older women. Baby Le-

Roy is left to the tender care of Tammany Young, who, to Fields' horror, amuses the tot by sending him scooting through the air across the store in one of those old-fashioned suspended cages once used for transporting small packages and change from one end of the store to another. Retrieved from the cage, within minutes LeRoy has removed the cork from a barrel of molasses, and the store is flooded with sticky syrup.

"I told him I wouldn't do it if I was him!" is Tammany Young's sincere explanation. Mrs. Dunk returns to rescue her child, promising never to bring her business to that store again.

That night, Fields has trouble sleeping, and the nagging of his wife, complaining about her years of suffering and hard work, doesn't help. Just as Fields is at the point of falling asleep, the phone rings.

"Well, why don't you answer the phone?" demands the tyrant. "I have no maid, you know; probably never will have!" Sleepily, Fields goes to the phone, but it is a wrong number: somebody calling for the maternity hospital. Mrs. Bissonette mulls this over for a minute, then: "Funny they should call *you* from the maternity hospital in the middle of the night." Fields mumbles an explanation. "No, dear, it was someone trying to *get* the maternity hospital." By now Mrs. Bissonette's sarcastic ire is fully aroused: "Oh, now you change it! Don't make it any worse by lying about it!"

As her tirade flows on, Fields gathers a pillow and blanket and heads for a more peaceful night on the porch outside. But the hammock is sadly in need of repair; it grunts and groans under Fields' weight, lurches unexpectedly, and squeaks like an army of mice. And so the night wears on into the early dawn. The milkman, with his rattling bottles, leaves a curious order for the tenants on the top floor—milk, cornflakes and a huge coconut. The coconut is of an exploratory nature, and ambles—bump, bump, bump—down the stairs, where it rattles around in an overturned garbage can before continuing its descent.

To all the intrusions on Fields' slumber by supposedly inanimate objects now is added a human one. At the foot of the back stairs appears a dapper young man, that excellent and personable comedian T. Roy Barnes, something of a far more stylish Bob Hope, who was never used to his full potential in movies. With an open, friendly smile, he yells up to Fields that he is looking for a Karl LaFong. To make sure that Fields has absorbed the name, he spells it out for him—capital K, small a, small r, small l, capital L, small a, capital F, small o, small n, small g. No, Fields counters, he doesn't know any Karl LaFong—spelling out each letter himself—"and if I did, I wouldn't admit it!"

With one bound, the interloper—now revealed as the apotheosis of all glib, fast-talking high-pressure salesmen—is up the stairs. "I'd say you were a man about fifty. . . ." he begins.

"Yes," mutters Fields, "you would say that!"

Barnes outlines the advantages of his insurance policies and all the extra benefits that accrue if one doesn't die until past the hundred-year mark. Fields is about to give him the heave-ho when Mrs. Bissonette appears at the window. "If you must exchange ribald stories with your friend, then have him come up at a reasonable hour." In vain, Fields protests that he doesn't even know the man. "Then why invite him up here?" is her exasperated comeback as she slams the window shut. Getting rid of the salesman doesn't ensure Fields any peace, however. Baby LeRoy is awake by now and, from the floor above, dropping grapes through a convenient knot-hole. They land squarely in Fields' open mouth, one after the other, almost choking him. "Shades of Bacchus!" he breathes, but this time it is an ice-pick that descends, quivering in the woodwork a fraction of an inch from his head.

With pardonable wrath, Fields rushes upstairs to confront the adorable little horror, but by now Mrs. Dunk has come out on to her porch and protects her offspring. She glares at Fields as Baby LeRoy coos innocently from the cradle of her arms, and berates him with "First you try to drown him in molasses, and now you try to poison him with filthy grapes!"

Returning to his hammock, Fields still has hopes of getting a short nap, but these hopes are doomed by the rasping squeaks as a neighbor hauls her wash on the clothesline. "Good morning, Mrs. Frobisher," Fields remarks offhandedly as a huge pair of bloomers is yanked into his field of vision. Mrs. Dunk's pretty but vapid young daughter descends the wooden stairs with a great clatter, but at the bottom remembers that she hasn't been given certain specific instructions. She yells back to her mother, who is now manicuring her nails on the top porch, to ask which of two drugstores she should go to and which of two almost identical brands of cough medicine she should buy.

Mother whines that she doesn't care, just get what is easiest. "I don't care either," whines back daughter, "you tell me where to go, and that's where I'll go!"

After minutes of this ear-grating chatter, Fields mutters to himself, "I know where I'd tell her to go!" This gives Mrs. Dunk her exit line. "It's no good, dear. I can't hear you. There's someone shouting on the floor below." The exchange also brings Mrs. Bissonette back into action. "What were you and that woman talking about?" she demands suspiciously. "Seems to me you've been getting very friendly with her lately!" Further discussion is aborted by the arrival of a noisy fruit peddler. Fields finally has had enough. He rushes into the house and comes out with a shotgun. "Vegetable man . . ." he calls enticingly. "Oh, vegetable gentleman. . . ." But the vendor has taken off. It is now broad daylight, everyone is awake, and presumably a state of sleepy lethargy will now descend upon the back porch for the rest of the day.

Soon the family is off to California by auto, over Mrs. Bissonette's predictions of dire disaster. The story is now too far along for much to be made of the cross-country trip, although there is some effective slapstick when Fields bounces the car across a plowed field, and in a gentle and charming overnight stay in a trailer camp. Fields, told to make up the fire and then fold the deck chair, becomes enmeshed in the confusing mechanics of the chair, disgustedly uses it as fuel for the

A Baby LeRoy-inspired flood closes the store; "It's a Gift." (Courtesy of Paramount Pictures)

fire, and amiably joins in some camp-fire singing. The bellowed "Moo!" of a cow jolts him from his content and with an obedient "Coming dear!" he goes back to the family tent.

Next day, they seek a quiet dell for a picnic. A charming-looking park catches their eye and they drive in, unaware that this is the private estate of a snooty millionaire and that the gate was open only because the guard was at that moment chasing away other trespassers. Fields drives into the grounds and collides with a marble statue of the Venus de Milo. "She walked right in front of the car!" he protests.

Making themselves at home, they soon have the lovely park in a shambles, strewn with empty paper bags, cans and other debris. Attempting to open a tomato can with a hatchet, Fields smears himself and the surrounding terrain with a shower of squashed tomatoes. Junior, wolfing down his sandwiches, wants more. "No!" says his mother firmly, and then adds "Take one of your father's." Fields obligingly offers half a sandwich, having first folded the meat over so that there is a double layer of meat in his half and merely two pieces of bread for junior.

The family dog begins to feel its oats a little, too, and sinks its teeth into a pillow. Junior's attempts to wrest away the pillow result in its being rent to shreds, and a snowfall of feathers is added to the already desecrated landscape.

Fields is more concerned with spitting feathers out of his sandwiches than with the damage that has been wrought, but Mrs. Bissonette is most upset. "Those were my mother's feathers!" she cries in despair. "Really?" perks up Fields, suddenly interested. "I didn't know your mother had any feathers." The orgy of devastation is brought to a halt by the arrival of the owner of the estate. Fields and family beat a hasty retreat, first driving their car into the sprinkler system and providing a downpour of water to add soggy havoc to all the debris they have left behind.

Driving toward their new home, Mrs. Bissonette finds her spirits rising in the California sunshine, and noticing all the fruitful orange groves, she feels that perhaps after all she has misjudged her husband. "I knew you had, dear. I just didn't want to say so," he replies humbly. They stop by the ranch of a stranger to ask directions. He is to be their new neighbor; their ranch is just down the road. Happily, they speed on their way—to be greeted by a tumbledown wreck of a shack that looks like a set from a road-company "Tobacco Road," surrounded by barren, dusty ground.

"Evidently a young orange tree," Fields muses, fingering one small scraggly plant that has somehow survived, and hopefully trying to find some asset in this dust bowl. As the ranch house proceeds to fall apart in his hands, Fields concedes that it will need a little fixing up. Mrs. Bissonette's worst fears have been realized and she announces her intention of taking daughter and junior and heading for the nearest town. The automobile, having performed gallantly in its cross-country hop, now collapses in a heap, and they have to leave on foot. As Fields sits there, stunned, succor arrives from an unexpected source. The neighbor from down the road rushes up to tell him that a multi-million-dollar raceway is about to be constructed, and that his land, while worthless for orange-growing, is essential to the new structure, since it is the only place where a grandstand can be built and not be in the full glare of the sun. "Don't let them bluff you," he winds up. "You can get *any* price!"

Scarcely has Fields absorbed this information when the real-estate operator arrives with his entourage. He turns out to be the same gentleman whose personal estate Fields has just reduced to a garbage heap, but business is business, and bygones are bygones as the two men square off for the fray.

At first, the millionaire denigrates the property, and magnanimously offers to pay Fields whatever *he* paid for it. Mrs. Bissonette, returning at this point, pleads with her husband to accept the deal, but for once he is deaf to her insistence. Firmly setting her down out of harm's way, he lets the bidding go on. Nonchalantly he turns down offers which have his poor wife squirming in anguish. Finally, admitting defeat, the real-estate man asks him what he wants for the land. Without flinching, Fields names an astronomical figure, amends it upward

—so that his friendly neighbor can have a commission—and also includes, as part of the deal, the best local orange grove that money can buy.

The buyer tries to come back with a lower counter-offer. "You're crazy!" retorts Fields. "And you're drunk!" snaps the buyer. "Yes," agrees Fields, "but I'll be sober tomorrow, and you'll be crazy for the rest of your life!"

The deal is made, and Mrs. Bissonette is slowly brought to her senses and to the realization of the triumphant coup pulled off by her husband. Fade out, and fade in to some time later. Fields is lording it over his orange grove, while the rest of the family, well dressed and riding in the latest and most luxurious limousine, head for town to spend some of the loot. Fields sits happily on the veranda of his new home, lazily reaches up to pick an orange from the nearest tree, squirts a minuscule portion of juice into his glass, fills it up with a generous slug of whisky, and settles back with a contented sigh.

One wonders if the self-satisfaction of this quiet final scene reflected Fields' own knowledge that he had finally made a perfect comedy. Incredibly, the reviews of the time were no more enthusiastic than they had been for lesser Fields films, and even suggested that Fields couldn't last much longer if he wasn't given worth-while material. *The New York Times* considered it merely a journeyman piece of work, while one respected critic termed the film crude, clumsy and amateurish.

Perhaps in those days when the comedy field was so much richer, standards were proportionately higher, but even so any casual dismissal of the film which contained that superbly creative and mathematically precise sleeping-porch episode seems beyond belief. Fields' caustic wisecrack to the millionaire—"I'll be sober tomorrow, but you'll always be crazy"—seems particularly apt when applied against his sniping critics. Most of their writings, and their names, have been forgotten; Fields can only seem funnier as the years go by.

"It's a Gift" is one of the most realistic of Fields' films, containing no impossible sight gags, little actual slapstick, and comparatively little exaggeration of human characteristics. The whining Dunks and the pompous Fitchmueller, to say nothing of the cross old Mr. Muckle—the kind of man one automatically resents precisely because he has an affliction and thereby must be afforded a sympathy he otherwise wouldn't deserve—are all recognizable, everyday types. Fields' observation of them is human and even a little affectionate, but it is acidly accurate. Permanently entrenched as a lasting classic, not only of Fields' art but of the art of screen comedy generally, "It's a Gift" also, like some of the better Laurel and Hardy comedies, offers a trenchant commentary on the manners and mores of the American Family of the thirties.

*Frustration, anguish, resignation. Fields, already late for the wrestling matches;
"Man on the Flying Trapeze."* (Courtesy of Paramount Pictures)

☞ 12.

1935: Charles Dickens, Booth Tarkington—and Charles Bogle

1935 gave W. C. Fields his only film at Metro-Goldwyn-Mayer, and his only starring "straight" acting role—that is, if one can conceive of his Micawber in "David Copperfield" as being radically different from his normal screen characters. The role as originally discussed by producer David Selznick and director George Cukor was considered better suited to a dramatic actor than to a comedian. Charles Laughton had been approached and, surprisingly, turned the part down. Fields was listed first in a cast that included such MGM reliables as Lionel Barrymore and Lewis Stone, and in a way this was justified, for his was the only major role that continued right through the film. (The Copperfield role was, of course, split in half, with Freddie Bartholomew playing David as a boy, and Frank Lawton, David as a young man.)

It was a happy choice all around, for not only did Fields wear his Dickensian costume perfectly, making Micawber a visual misfit as well as a social one, but the role of the kindly, harried but mildly dishonest husband was a further extension of the screen role with which Fields was already identified. The part was temperamentally congenial, since, although Micawber appears and reappears constantly throughout the movie, he is not called upon for sustained involvement with the plot or the other characters. With so many characters, incidents and subplots in the script, any Fieldsian capers and demands for re-writes could be handled —with tact, diplomacy and probably outright lies—without holding up shooting.

Fields was incensed at not being allowed to work his juggling routines into the proceedings, and pointed out that Dickens had neglected to write such a sequence into the book only because he hadn't happened to think of it, not having had a show business background. Despite the soundness of this reasoning, and the possibility that a juggling Micawber could have been faithful to the spirit if not the letter of the original, the point was not well received by the MGM front office, which was notoriously less flexible than Paramount's. The juggling stayed out, but Micawber-Fields still had difficulty in donning his stovepipe hat without its first finding its way onto his upraised cane!

Although a "safe" and cinematically not too inventive adaptation, "David Copperfield" was so tastefully and handsomely made and so splendidly acted (especially by the then less familiar British imports, notably Hugh Williams as Steerforth) that it was to remain the best film evocation of Dickens until David Lean's "Great Expectations" and "Oliver Twist" in the forties.

From English literature Fields returned to Americana. His next assignment was the third movie version of Booth Tarkington's "Magnolia," this time under the title "Mississippi" (previous titles: "The Fighting Coward," in early 1924, and "River of Romance," in 1928). If this was one of Fields' lesser vehicles, it was primarily because his role as the blustering showboat "Commodore" was naturally a secondary one, and it suffered from attempts to blow it up to larger proportions. Given its right perspective, the part was foolproof, and any actor worth his salt could have used it to steal scenes right and left. Veteran thief Ernest Torrence did just that in the 1924 version, mugging beautifully with his magnificently craggy face, and deftly taking snuff or flourishing a huge handkerchief every time the official star, Cullen Landis (who never had a chance!), was to have taken over the limelight.

Realizing that the role was good, and that he had monopolized all the best comedy opportunities, Fields must have been startled indeed to find that the cool and easygoing assurance of Bing Crosby was reversing the historic procedure and taking the picture away from him. Crosby, in addition to his own abilities, had a great deal going for him in "Mississippi," including some charming love scenes with Joan Bennett and a really rugged fist battle with Fred Kohler, Sr. (This was well before the era when the studios tried to masculinize their pretty-boy heroes, like Robert Taylor and Nelson Eddy, by pitting them against Wallace Beery and Victor McLaglen in fight scenes.) Most of all, Crosby had some of Rodgers and Hart's loveliest songs to sing, including "Down by the River" and "It's Easy to Remember."

132

The plot, which may also have inspired Buster Keaton's classic silent, "Our Hospitality," spoofs the Southern code of honor in general, and specifically the ritual of dueling. When Crosby refuses to duel over a trivial matter, he is disgraced, ordered to leave the house of his fiancee (Gail Patrick), and apparently loses her love too. She is a fickle young belle, and has a kid sister (Joan Bennett) whose sincere love for Crosby won't be realized and reciprocated until the final reel.

Crosby, convinced by showboat impresario Fields that the only way to avoid trouble is to create such a reputation for toughness that no one will dare provoke an argument, joins the showboat troupe and is systematically turned into a big attraction under the billing of "The Singing Killer." Ultimately, of course, his courage—which is never really in doubt—is proved, the aristocratic Rumford family are forced to eat humble pie, and there's a romantic fadeout for Crosby and the younger sister, now nicely grown up.

Visually a handsome production, with stylish groupings and interesting camera angles (especially in the earlier sequences in the Rumford mansion), the film is more than a little disjointed, certain sequences tailing off abruptly or failing to build as promised, so that one suspects a good deal of post-production editorial tampering. Possibly it was thought that the mixture of charm and subtlety (from the original) and the more traditional Fieldsian humor didn't mix, and in view of the great personal success that Crosby was scoring, attempts may have been made to divert the film even more in his direction. Billing him above Fields indicates this.

Nevertheless, there was quite enough of the expected Fields humor—mainly verbal this time—to keep his fans quite happy. At the helm of his showboat, he puffs furiously at his cigar, lifting it delicately every so often by a flick of his tongue to avoid the spokes of the wheel when he changes direction. Frequently he extols the medicinal values of liquor for himself ("I've never been afraid of liquor in my life!") but is at pains to restrict its use by others.

"No more, you've had enough," he remarks at one point, having offered a restorative sip to a friend who has been slugged.

There is the inevitable poker game, at which he cheats outrageously, and frequent opportunities for his "Mother of Pearl!" and other time-honored expletives. He is at his best in rambling accounts of his one-man battles against hordes of savage Indians. "There I was . . . my canoe under one arm, a Rocky mountain goat under the other. . . . I took my knife and carved a path through a wall of living flesh . . . dragging my canoe behind me!" A spellbound listener asks him what happened to the goat. "Ah, he was very good with mustard!" answers Fields.

Toward the end of the film, he faces another audience and asks hopefully if he has ever told them about his experiences with the Indians. Yes, he has, they reply firmly. Only momentarily crestfallen, he comes back with "Well, I didn't tell you all the details—" Once again he recounts how he carved his path through that wall of living flesh. His attention diverted by an Indian staring at him through the port-hole—actually it is a wooden cigar-store Indian—Fields rapidly switches his tale from one of blood-thirsty vengeance to the theme of brotherhood: "Shortly after that, of course, the noble redman and his paleface friend smoked the pipe of peace."

Many of Fields' choicest gags are little more than throwaways, designed to wrap up a Crosby sequence, as, for example, a poker brawl, which Crosby settles himself. Fields quickly grabs a pair of pistols, blows cigar smoke down the barrels, and with his smoking guns as evidence, modestly takes the credit for the bodies huddled on the floor. One of his most effective exits occurs after Crosby sings "Swanee River." Fields snorts at the song and predicts its failure: "It's no good . . . it'll be forgotten in two weeks . . . people can't remember the tune!" And he jauntily walks off, humming it.

With due respect to Charles Dickens and Booth Tarkington, the best Fields script of 1935 was one that he wrote himself, as Charles Bogle, in collaboration with his actor-comedian-writer friend Sam Hardy. The film, "The Man on the Flying Trapeze," was not a circus story, nor did its title have the remotest connection, even symbolically, with anything that went on during its tight sixty-five minutes. Although not quite up to the superb standards of "It's a Gift," it was still top-flight Fields, and was to be his last major work until "The Bank Dick" in 1940.

Despite gleefully sadistic onslaughts against wives, sons, daughters and clinging relatives in other films, both before and afterward, "Flying Trapeze" was his apotheosis of the American Family. Since Fields rarely did anything by accident, especially not the aiming of his most barbed arrows, one can assume that there was more than a little personal satisfaction and malice in the casting of roly-poly Grady Sutton as his thoroughly shiftless brother-in-law, and calling him Claude—the name of Fields' own son. His once happy marriage had long since gone on the rocks, and he was to remain estranged from his wife and son for the rest of his life.

It must be observed that after his death they behaved in a manner quite in keeping with Fields' notions of how all wives and sons behaved, descending on his estate, putting his will into litigation, slicing up and whittling away at the fortune he had so carefully amassed through the years, and even overruling some purely personal requests.*

*   These facts are quoted with acknowledgment to Robert Lewis Taylor and W. C. *Fields, His Follies and Fortunes* (Doubleday: 1949). The last chapter of that book cites many other saddening examples of his last wishes being totally disregarded. Taylor writes: "Fields' will stipulated that his body was to be taken to a cemetery and immediately cremated, and that under no conditions was he to have any sort of a funeral. He had three. Mrs. Fields indicated that she would overrule the comedian's wish about cremation, on the ground that such a procedure was contrary to her religious doctrines. No mention was made of Fields' doctrines. In the scrapping over his money, Fields himself was largely forgotten. Two years after his death he lay in an unmarked grave."

Fields—still unquestionably Fields—as Mr. Micawber; "David Copperfield."
(Courtesy of Metro-Goldwyn-Mayer)

In another way, too, "The Man on the Flying Trapeze" was oddly prophetic. Playing a small role was Carlotta Monti, a pretty young Mexican actress whom Fields had befriended earlier in the thirties, and who was to remain a devoted and loyal friend, nursing him through his long periods of illness, remaining at his bedside until the moment of his death in 1946. In "Flying Trapeze" she played his secretary—an adoring, devoted, respectful secretary.

The part is small, yet even if one were not aware of their personal relationship, it is strangely touching. Toward the end of the picture, when Fields is being attacked on all sides by family and business associates, it is Miss Monti who rushes to his defense with an impassioned outburst. Whether she could ever have developed into an actress of note had she not devoted herself and her time to Fields' welfare is debatable; she probably had no more nor less talent than Susan Fleming, the dark-haired beauty of "Million Dollar Legs" who did try for a career and never made it.

But Carlotta Monti's scenes in "The Man on the Flying Trapeze" draw a poignant parallel to her off-screen devotion to Fields. To her, and probably not by accident, goes the single funniest moment in the film—a remarkable outburst of pure Fieldsian verbiage, which becomes hilariously funny through the seriousness of her delivery. If Miss Monti was striving for mock gravity, then she had a brilliant sense of humor and it is sad indeed that she wasn't used more in movies. But, in all probability, merely remembering the sublime idiocies of such a speech was such an effort that deliberate attempts at humorous delivery would have been beyond the reach of a Lombard or a Colbert. In any event, it is the film's real climax, and Fields wisely doesn't attempt to top it himself—except for the discomfitures of Claude and his mother-in-law that the audience has been waiting for too patiently to be denied.

It is evening in the home of Ambrose Wolfinger. His wife is once more that magnificently supercilious martyr, Kathleen Howard. Ambrose is in the bathroom taking his nightcap, which has to be hidden in the medicine cabinet. "What are you doing in there?" imperiously demands his wife. Ambrose hurriedly swallows another shot and reaches for his toothbrush. "Just brushing my teeth, dear," he tells her patiently, gargling with it as the next skeptical question is hurled: "Are you *sure* you're brushing your teeth?" Ambrose walks back to the bedroom like a somnambulist. Obviously this nightly inquisition is old-stuff now. He is too tired and basically too good-hearted to argue back, and he finds it easier to roll with the punches.

Sitting on the bed, he removes one sock, blows into it, folds it neatly and then, noticing a fly on his pillow, executes it with a mighty blow from the flyswatter.

"What are you doing *now?*" moans his wife.

"Er—taking off my socks, dear!" he tells her soothingly.

But repose is doomed: burglars break into the cellar (one of them a youthful Walter Brennan), discover a keg of applejack, and, having sampled it, launch

136

into a chorus of "On the Banks of the Wabash." Mrs. Wolfinger is instantly aroused, and fearful for the fate of "poor, helpless mother" in the next room. Reluctantly Fields arises, not really too concerned about the burglars, but unable to persuade his wife that they can be dealt with in the morning.

He carefully unfolds his socks, puts one on his right foot, and then absent-mindedly pulls the other one on over it. There is a delay while he searches for second sock, and time out to beat another fly into oblivion. Looking in a drawer to find his gun, he finds instead another welcome delaying tactic—"Here are those gloves you lost!"

Eventually, he is forced to take out the gun and prepare for action. The shouting from the cellar increasing, his now thoroughly scared mother-in-law, Mrs. Nesselrode (played by that lovable old wreck of a busybody, Vera Lewis), bursts into the bedroom. Startled, Fields lets fly with his pistol, shooting in her general direction. "Did I kill you?" he inquires hopefully, the question tailing off despairingly when he realizes that he has missed.

Both women now urge him to investigate disturbances in the cellar. Fields thinks that brother-in-law Claude should accompany him, but Mrs. Nesselrode will have none of such a selfish thought; Claude might get killed, and she would be left all alone. The thought so frightens her that she almost faints, and Fields hastens to revive her by offering a liquid stimulant. Her puritanical zeal reviving her instead, she tells him coyly, "When I was a young and pretty girl, I promised my mother that liquor would never touch my lips." Fields looks unconvinced, but doesn't make an issue of it.

"Pretty sentiment, mother," he murmurs with just a trace of sarcasm, and decides that perhaps he should brush his teeth again before tackling the marauders below. Then—an inspiration—he decides to call the local protective patrol association to which he is a paid-up subscriber. Understandably a little nervous, he calls the wrong number and a woman answers. "Who was that woman?" demands his wife. Unsatisfied with the explanation that it was just Mrs. Crud and a wrong number, she wonders just how long this has been going on.

Fields gets the right number, ascertains that help is on the way, and then—despite the admonitions of his daughter (Mary Brian), the only member of his family who genuinely loves him, is happy to escape to the doubtless more congenial company of the bandits downstairs.

His descent is not so stealthy as he had planned; a trip at the top of the cellar stairs and a spectacular fall land him on a sharp nail, which he pries loose from his derrière with an agonized "Drat!" Recovering his wits and his gun, he orders the intruders to take their filthy hands off his liquor. But they turn out to be likeable fellows, and in no time at all three voices from the cellar rise in song to the waiting women.

The arrival of the patrolman precipitates another spectacular fall on his head for Fields, whose unnaturally restrained "Oh dear!" speaks more than volumes of profanity. Ambrose is prepared to drop the whole thing and let these fellows go, but the policeman will have none of it; this is the first call he has had in weeks, and he needs to justify his job. Fields and the burglars are marched down to the lock-up; the applejack is brought along as evidence, the three are still singing. Between songs the policeman asks Fields for the time. An outraged voice bawls, "Cut out that singing—don't you know it's five in the morning?" "It's five o'clock," Fields tells the patrolman.

The judge on night duty seems more interested in cause than in effect. "Got a permit for that applejack?" he snarls at Fields. "I guess I could get one easily enough," Fields responds in an amiable manner.

The two drunken burglars are set free, but Fields is incarcerated in a cell with a bearded homicidal maniac whose conscience is prompting him to re-enact several crimes of passion. His most recent indiscretion has been to murder his wife by stabbing her in the neck with a pair of scissors, but, as he is at pains to point out, she was the first wife that he had ever killed.

"Oh, well, that's in your favor," agrees Fields, in a matter-of-fact tone that suggests instant acquittal by any fair-minded jury.

At home, the news of Ambrose's incarceration is received with great glee by all but his daughter, who takes her meager savings down to the jail to bail him out. With misguided loyalty, she does not correct Fields when he assumes that his wife has sent down the bail money. "She's pretty nice about things like that," he reflects. "Other things she's not so nice about."

There is a cold reception waiting for him at breakfast; his brother-in-law Claude calls him a jail-bird, his wife pointedly avoids his kiss, and all of the food is gone—or is being reserved for Claude. "Are you going to eat the rest of that sausage?" Fields inquires timidly of his wife, reaching out for the small remaining slice pushed to one side of her plate. "Yes I am!" she snaps, spearing it with her fork. All that is left is cold dry toast, but Fields is philosophical about this: "I've been eating cold toast for eight years now . . . I kind of like it."

The suggestion of a happy smile lights up Mrs. Wolfinger's face. She has found a new avant-garde poem in the paper. "We have what we have not . . ." she begins, pausing to let it sink in and to make sure that her husband is listening appreciatively. Satisfied that he is, she reads it all to him, the stream of meaningless words interrupted occasionally by the crunch of very dry toast. When she has finished, she puts the paper down triumphantly and sums up with "And the beautiful part of it is there's no punctuation!"

Life is currently bearable for Ambrose only because he is a great wrestling fan, and the match of the season between Tossoff and Mishabobb is due in a couple of days. He has secured a fifteen-dollar front-row ticket and is determined in some way to get the afternoon off from work. However, he is more than a little chagrined when Claude proudly announces that he has just found a fifteen-dollar front-row ticket and Ambrose discovers that his own is missing—the more so since he cannot explain such extravagance to his wife, and has to let the prized ticket go to Claude by default.

In scene cut from film before release, David Copperfield bids farewell to Micawbers, who are going to Australia. (Courtesy of Metro-Goldwyn-Mayer)

Later, in his office, he is surprised to find that his secretary, Carlotta Monti, is also a fight fan, and furthermore that her mother is a close personal friend of one of the contestants, Kulabosh Mishabobb. Ambrose is most impressed; "I never knew his first name," he murmurs. But there is no time for more discussion; Ambrose is summoned to the office of his boss, Mr. Malloy, played by Oscar Apfel.

Mr. Malloy is mildly irked; where was Wolfinger this morning when Malloy needed him? Ambrose is abjectly apologetic. He was sent to the bank very early, and had to wait in line until it opened at nine o'clock. Ambrose's disorganized habits are tolerated because his fantastic memory is one of the firm's major public-relations assets, and Malloy wants to call on it today.

A big Australian client, one J. Frothingham Wallaby, is due, and Malloy cannot remember anything about him. Ambrose's card-index mind immediately springs into action, and he recalls Mr. Wallaby's last visit, some five years earlier, with almost embarrassing clarity. "Wallaby . . . has two boys . . . one of them is a champion tennis player, but the other one is a manly little fellow. . . ." To such useful personal details, Ambrose adds an account of Malloy's last business meeting with Wallaby, which wound up in a speakeasy with a drunken Indian potentate in tow and some young ladies' garters in Malloy's pockets.

Malloy hurriedly sends Ambrose back to his desk, where a fellow clerk seeks his aid. Somewhere in the office there is a letter from a Swedish client, written some four years ago, which must be produced immediately. Ambrose studies the litter-strewn roll-top desk which comprises his filing system, mentally sorts out which pile of papers represents Scandinavian territories of four years ago, plunges his hand into the mess, and comes out with precisely the right piece of correspondence.

Having proved his worth twice in rapid succession, he feels that now might be an opportune time to ask for the afternoon off. Though he has never taken any time off in his twenty-five years with the firm, as a conscientious employee he feels that he hardly should ask to be excused for personal pleasure. Perhaps if he were to ask permission to attend a funeral. . . .

Malloy is most sympathetic when Ambrose relates the sad tale of his mother-in-law's death. "What did she die of?" he inquires sympathetically. "Who?" asks Fields, so unaccustomed to lying that he hasn't thought out his plan very carefully. But having gone this far, he has to go the rest of the way, so he concocts a story of Mrs. Nesselrode's demise through excessive use of bad alcohol. Malloy, who is an understanding boss, is deeply moved.

"It must be hard to lose your mother-in-law," he says.

"Yes, it is," confirms Ambrose. "Very hard. Almost impossible."

The ruse works and Ambrose—minus the ticket that Claude has purloined—is off to the fights. He reckons without the belligerence of the California police force, however, and on this particular day they are out to get him. For a fancied infringement, cop number one orders Fields to pull over to the curb—even though this entails stopping in a "No Parking" zone and, quite incidentally, wrecking the parked motorcycle of cop number two.

The first ticket written, cop number one leaves, but Fields' departure is now blocked by a huge packing crate. Before it can be removed, the owner of the demolished motorcycle arrives, his block of tickets at the ready. In vain Fields insists that he was told by cop number one to pull into a "No Parking" zone and forced to wreck the unfortunate motorcycle. The sarcastic cop isn't buying this, and since everything Fields says makes the situation that much worse, Fields decides to knuckle under to the fates and take what comes without further defense.

After making Fields read the "No Parking" sign—slowly, deliberately and several times—to make sure that he understands, Fields obeying in a tone of meek humility, the cop issues his tickets to Fields and orders him to move on. The crate has now been removed, but another hazard is created as an expensive limousine draws up behind Fields. He goes into reverse and crashes into the limousine, whose chauffeur—the always tough and irascible James Flavin—loses no time in telling Fields just what he thinks of him. Recognizing the futility of fighting destiny, Fields settles down to the reading of his newspaper until such time as all exits are clear for him.

With the precision of a Greek tragedy, the battered limousine drives off only seconds before cop number two rounds the corner again, to be greeted by the sight of Fields sitting nonchalantly in his auto, reading the newspaper in a zone still very clearly marked "No Parking." During the ensuing and even more heart-rending argument, Fields is served with more tickets, and backs up once more. This time an ambulance is the obstacle, and as Fields' car collides with it, the patient on the stretcher is ejected from the rear door and sails merrily down the street. The patient's mother—or wife—is an excitable Italian woman who adds her torrent of verbal abuse to the inquisition of the traffic cops.

Mercifully the scene cuts away to Ambrose's home, where mysterious wreaths of flowers are arriving. Thinking perhaps, and without too much concern, that Ambrose has met with a fatal accident, his wife calls the office. Peabody, Ambrose's prissy immediate superior (well played by Lucien Littlefield), reveals that he has learned the sad news that Mrs. Nesselrode has just passed away from alcoholic poisoning. Sympathetic friends in the office are responsible for the floral tributes, and also for releasing the full details of Mrs. Nesselrode's demise to the newspapers.

Mrs. Wolfinger declares that her mother is very much alive, and Peabody, rubbing his hands, is delighted, for here is an ideal excuse to fire Ambrose.

Meanwhile, Ambrose, having made his escape from the "No Parking" quicksand, is in more trouble. While he is trying to change a flat tire and argue with a belligerent fellow motorist at the same time, his spare rolls away down an almost perpendicular hill.

Fields gives chase, narrowly avoiding sundry trucks and streetcars on the busy highway, and reaches a high train trestle, where locomotives are passing in opposite directions just as the tire lures its pursuer on to the trestle. (This particular location is a familiar landmark in Hollywood slapstick comedy, and was in frequent use after Sennett first discovered its possibilities in 1916.)

Hardly a convincing sequence, this makes maximum use of doubles for Fields, back-projected effects, and even some incredibly obvious treadmill scenes on the locomotive trestle itself. However, the sheer audacity with which Fields used such mechanical trickery was funny in itself, and the laughs come mainly from Fields' grace and nonchalance as he skips and hops from one track to the other, barely avoiding the huge iron horses that thunder up behind him as he, all unawares, concentrates on catching the elusive tire.

Here, where the gag stresses Fields' imperturbability and is shot mostly in closeups, the obvious faking is almost an asset. (Similar over-use of back projection in a Laurel and Hardy car chase sequence for "County Hospital" failed completely, since the aim was comedy and thrill, and without visual conviction there was no thrill.)

When Fields gets to the wrestling arena, he is the last of a long line of fans waiting at the box office, and the cashier slams the "Sold Out" sign in his face just as he eagerly steps up to the window. The preliminaries are over, the big Mishabobb and Tossoff battle is about to begin, and Fields in desperation tries to get at least a glimpse of this long-awaited struggle through a knot-hole. But now the battle is almost finished. One mighty antagonist grapples with the other, whirls him around, and heaves him out of the ring. The huge body flies through the air and out of the arena, where it collides with poor Ambrose and knocks him to the sidewalk.

His faithful secretary, who has been seeing the wrestling matches, too, rushes to his aid. And Claude, emerging with the rest of the crowd, is delighted. "Drunk again, and lying in the gutter!" he proclaims in triumph. He rushes home to tell Mrs. Wolfinger and her mother, who still are trying to dig themselves out from under a welter of wreaths for Mrs. Nesselrode and to adjust to the tidings that their breadwinner has been fired from his job.

Claude is overjoyed to find that his gossip can top even their news. Suggesting that Ambrose and his secretary have been conducting bacchanalian orgies, he reveals that they have drunk themselves into a stupor and fallen together into the gutter, a public disgrace that can never be lived down. The elder ladies are not in the least surprised; daughter Hope doesn't believe a word of it.

Grimy and wilted, Fields makes his entrance carrying a small bunch of flowers. "A little nosegay!" he booms ingratiatingly to his wife, who tosses it aside to become lost among the funeral wreaths. Fields is contrite, but having missed the fight and lost his job, he is in no mood to be badgered. He admits to being wrong in lying in order to get the afternoon off, but that is all.

His temper is slowly rising, but his wife and mother-in-law cannot believe that the worm is finally turning, and they continue to bait him. Unable to stand it any longer, he explodes, telling mother-in-law and her worthless son exactly what he thinks of them, and climaxing his tirade with a mighty haymaker that knocks Claude down for the count. Delighted to find so much satisfaction in letting off steam at last, he takes a wild swing at Mrs. Nesselrode too. Unfortunately it misses.

Back at the office there is turmoil. Another key customer, one Mr. Muckenback, is coming in, and Malloy needs the help of Ambrose's phenomenal memory. Peabody proudly announces that he has fired Ambrose, and Malloy is aghast. One doesn't fire a man for the first little slip he has made in twenty-five years. Very well, counters Peabody, but what about Ambrose's disgraceful behavior at the fight arena?

His loyal secretary can stand silent no longer, and in a speech of steadily mounting fury, indignation and passion, she tells the whole story and totally exonerates Ambrose—leaving herself and the entire assembly quite breathless with her eloquence and sheer lung power. "And so Kulabosh Mishabobb picked up

Fields as the intrepid skipper of the showboat; "Mississippi." (Courtesy of Paramount Pictures)

With Freddie Bartholomew as the young David, in "David Copperfield."
(Courtesy of Metro-Goldwyn-Mayer)

Fields as Mr. Micawber, with Frank Lawton (David) and Roland Young (Uriah Heep) in "David Copperfield." (Courtesy of Metro-Goldwyn-Mayer)

Tossoff and threw Tossoff at poor Mr. Wolfinger, knocking him down," she concludes. "What was I to do, let my employer die there in the gutter?"

Malloy is ordered to get Ambrose back or else—and promptly gets the Wolfinger home on the phone. It is Ambrose's daughter who takes the call, and she is unimpressed by Peabody's smug offers to let bygones be bygones and permit Ambrose to return to his old job and his old salary. A true daughter of a Fieldsian father, she concocts a fantastic yarn about a super-lucrative contract, including long paid vacations, currently being offered to her father by Moe Litvak of the Irish Woolen Mills.

Over a barrel, Peabody agrees to meet the terms, while Ambrose, who hasn't been taking in all of this, wonders if the old firm will take him back if he goes down and apologizes and agrees to take a reduction in salary.

The new financial standing of Ambrose makes a difference in the household. Mrs. Wolfinger somewhat unconvincingly sees the error of her ways and announces that she is going to be a much better wife from now on. Mrs. Nesselrode is told to get out, and Claude to get a job. However, they are not being cast off entirely, and to show that he still considers them part of the family, Ambrose takes them for a ride in his roadster, seating them in the rumble seat.

He is delighted when they are enveloped in a torrential downpour, and while he, Mrs. Wolfinger and daughter Hope enjoy a thermos of coffee, safe from the elements, he slows to a walking pace so that the shivering couple in the rumble seat can make the most of their exposure to such unusual California weather.

Fields obliges the cameraman: "You Can't Cheat an Honest Man." (Courtesy of Universal Pictures)

☞ 13.

The Last Days
at Paramount

1936 and 1937 were not happy years for Fields. He was no longer a young man, and the once rugged constitution could no longer stand the twin adversaries of abuse (primarily alcoholic) and neglect (Fields, hating doctors, called them only when absolutely necessary—and even then usually only to disregard their advice and to haggle over their fees). Inevitably, the doctors told him he must cut down on his alcohol consumption if he wanted to stay alive, and, equally inevitably, Fields did his best to increase that already quite staggering consumption in order to prove what fools and charlatans they were.

Fields was also saddened—and hardly encouraged in the contemplation of his own condition—by the deaths of three of his close friends, writer Jim Tully, character comedian Sam Hardy, and Will Rogers. For the first time a victim of delirium tremens, he also became more moody and suspicious of his fellow-men than ever, suspecting that marauders, bandits, thieves in the night and kidnappers were spending all of their waking hours dreaming up schemes to defraud or injure him. Unable to sleep at night, he devoted much of his time to a diligent study of news-

*Fields, after being hit by the flying body of a wrestler, with Carlotta Monti;
"Man on the Flying Trapeze."* (Courtesy of Paramount Pictures)

papers and periodicals in which he carefully marked for future reference and use
all items of a scandalous, obnoxious or horrifying nature, especially those which
related to such pet peeves as doctors, bankers and Negroes.

Fields made only two films in 1936-37, both of them under the shadow of
an illness so serious that it could have become critical at any moment. Although
a lengthy convalescence in the desert prior to shooting "Poppy" enabled him to
sustain himself during that film, a much longer illness—with pneumonia as one
of the complications—followed. Fields himself was well aware of the seriousness of
his condition, although he did little to alleviate it by cooperating with the doctors,
especially in the vital matter of his drinking.

During occasional periods of depression, he said that he didn't really expect
to live out the year, and that "the fellow in the bright nightgown" (Fields' own
description for Death) would most likely be collecting him at any time now.
Fields' sense of humor and his performing ability seem to have been affected not
at all during this low period. There is no sign in his films of any problems. Nothing on the screen even remotely suggests his desperate fight against sickness. It is

"A little nosegay," humbly offered to harsh wife (Kathleen Howard); "The Man on the Flying Trapeze." (Courtesy of Paramount Pictures)

only what is not shown on the screen that reveals something to be wrong. There are disproportionately long passages where the Fields character disappears completely, while the secondary leads take over the story-line; and Fields himself, especially in "Poppy," is seen in medium and long shots far more than usual. This was so that Fields' strength could be conserved for the dialogue and comedy business that only he could do, while a double could take over in the other shots.

Director Eddie Sutherland once estimated that Fields actually appeared only in about twenty-five percent of his scenes in "Poppy." Recent study of the film suggests that this estimate of the authentic Fields footage, made by Sutherland many years later, was low, but there is certainly no doubt that a double was used extensively, and that the script had been re-shuffled and new emphasis given to other characters in order to shoot around Fields as much as possible.

Considering the difficulties involved, "Poppy" turned out surprisingly well, though as a Fields vehicle, and more specifically as a re-make of the picture that had first brought Fields to fame, it inevitably disappointed. Despite the added advantage of sound in "Poppy," there still was probably more of the essence of

Eustace McGargle in the silent version, "Sally of the Sawdust." The original was simpler and less cluttered with characters who have to be both explained and then disposed of, although this stress on secondary roles (especially Lynne Overman as a shrewd hick lawyer) may be deliberate in order to occupy footage that would normally have gone to the star.

With these complications as well as the addition of songs, "Poppy" hewed reasonably well to its original story-line, and only in a stylistic sense did it differ very much from the Griffith film. It had no elements of melodrama and no chase finale, and its romantic sub-plot, though charming, was completely artificial. Poppy and her boy-friend—pleasingly played by Rochelle Hudson and Richard Cromwell—seemed as unrealistic in the milieu of the thirties as did the period story-line itself.

As if recognizing this, director Eddie Sutherland handled all of their love scenes on a Cinderella level of total unreality, which included some of the most elaborately artificial exterior sets of country lanes, meadows and riverside walks ever constructed. The whole film became a kind of fairy-tale, with an old-world sentimentality surprisingly (though perhaps unintentionally) akin to that of Griffith. In the Griffith version, the love scenes had been wholly naturalistic, played out entirely against authentic Connecticut exteriors.

Both films offered differing approaches to Fields' stage hit, while coming up with end results that were similar in spirit. The pity is that neither version really did justice to Fields' association with it, or gave him full rein in the McGargle role.

Nevertheless, "Poppy" afforded him some fine comedy highlights missing from the silent version, starting off with an episode in which Fields cunningly sells a "talking dog" to a sucker. After the deal is consummated, the new owner makes a remark at which Fields is quick to take unnecessary umbrage, and the dog huffily remarks that just for that, he'll never speak again.

"He probably means it, too," prophesies ventriloquist Fields as he leaves.

Fields, colorfully attired in white stovepipe hat, large spotted cravat, cutaway coat, checkered trousers and white spats, was a constant visual delight, especially when manipulating a croquet mallet, although this long-promised sequence tends to run down hill, and one suspects it was a casualty of Fields' infirmities.

Fields' last picture for Paramount, "The Big Broadcast of 1938," made in mid-1937, was one of his longest films and in many ways his most frustrating. Fields had never needed romantic sub-plots (other than those directly involving his own character, usually as father of the heroine) and he certainly never had needed song-and-dance guest stars. A large-scale musical extravaganza, "The Big Broadcast of 1938" desperately needed Fields to provide comedy and his authoritative personality to hold its rambling plot together. What story-line there was (three writers are credited with a screenplay taken from a Howard Lindsay and

Rochelle Hudson is Fields' adopted daughter in "Poppy." Granville Bates at right. (Courtesy of Paramount Pictures)

Russel Crouse adaptation of an original by yet a sixth writer!) would have worked far better if it had been cut down to the bare bones and handled purely as a wacky comedy.

The Fields routines, emphasized at the beginning of the film and then spaced farther and farther apart, give indications of having been constructed pretty much by Fields himself or by an uncredited comedy director working with him; nevertheless, Fields must have been hampered by working with the director in charge of the picture, Mitchell Leisen, whose ideas were alien to Fields' work.

Leisen formerly had been a film art director, and his pictures have always looked as though they were made with visual elegance as the key consideration. When he has worked in comedy, Leisen has achieved a superficial imitation of Lubitsch; in drama or melodrama, he has sometimes adopted a moderately effective pseudo-Lang or -Sternberg style; but his own style—or lack of personal style—has always been artificial and décor-conscious.

Even the best Fields moments in "The Big Broadcast of 1938" too often seem diluted by getting lost in sets that distract the attention, or in the *chi-chi* em-

Fields with director Eddie Sutherland during the filming of "Poppy." (Courtesy of Paramount Pictures)

phasis on blank expanses of white in background décor. However, Fields was by no means the only casualty. Kirsten Flagstad was one of several singers signed for specialty "numbers," and while she actually performed two, only "Brunnhilde's Battlecry" from "The Valkyries" remained in the film. (Confirmed Flagstad fans got a bonus if they saw the trailer, since it included part of an aria deleted from the film itself.) Other diversionary sequences included some rather tiresome numbers by Tito Guizar; the pleasant "Thanks for the Memory," done by Bob Hope and Shirley Ross; and a cartoon episode created by Leon Schlesinger —rather curiously brought in from Warner Brothers, even though Paramount had their own house cartoonist in Max Fleischer.

"The Big Broadcast of 1938" was far from lacking in entertainment, and the elaborate special effects and miniature sequences (the story was built around a cross-ocean race between two giant liners) were diverting in themselves. But the film was top-heavy and ponderous, and completely lacked the spontaneous zaniness that had made "International House" so much fun even when Fields was kept off screen for long periods.

Despite the presumed foreknowledge that this would be Fields' last Paramount film, and the presence in the cast of a number of players that Paramount were grooming for stardom (Martha Raye, listed second in the cast, Dorothy Lamour third and Bob Hope strangely in sixth position, although he was the nominal leading man), Fields was given solo star billing, and was in fine form in his dual role as T. Frothingwell Bellows, millionaire playboy, and his slightly more serious brother, S. B. Bellows.

Frothingwell, on his way to play golf, stops at a service station to fill up his cigarette lighter, lights his cigar, and promptly demolishes the entire establishment with one mighty explosion.

The golf-course sequence which follows is such a top-notch sampling of pure Fieldsiana that the rest of the film—which is never again so generous with his footage—cannot top it. Followed by a squad of "yes-men" caddies, Frothingwell speeds around the course in a propeller-driven cart. Stopping at one point to remove his shoe and let a veritable mountain of sand pour from it, he murmurs "Ah, there's that plum sandwich now!"

Remembering that he has to be aboard the *Colossal* when it races the *Gigantic* to Cherbourg, he pulls the appropriate levers and his golf-cart turns into a miniature plane, taking off into the heavens to fly past a goose or two before overtaking the competing ships.

Once aboard ship, Fields' role is almost scuttled in favor of a romance between Leif Erikson and Dorothy Lamour; another sub-plot in which Bob Hope emerges from complications with various ex-wives to re-marry the one he really loves; a continuous floor-show, or rehearsals for it; and ultimately some extended and unfunny comedy routines with Martha Raye. (The basic premise of Miss Raye's role—that she crashed an airplane into a mirror factory, broke nine thousand mirrors and thus became a permanent jinx—is funny enough, but the gags resulting from it are predictable and labored.)

Fields saunters through the remainder of the film with vast self-assurance, delivering a superb throwaway line here, getting in a short routine there, but never being allowed sufficient footage to take command again.

He explains the ship's complicated electronic machinery, which he has never seen before in his life, to the assembled newsmen, and begins with the very heart of the mechanism: "That," he points out urbanely, "is a still."

Wandering around the decks, he makes ingratiatingly absurd remarks to pretty girls, tosses off irrelevant insults about Irishmen and pickaninnies, and, for one welcome oasis of visual comedy, does a variation on his old poolroom routine again.

Everything that he does and says is funny, showing him to be at the height of his powers despite his grave illness, but one-liners and quick bits of business do not suffice for Fields. Apart from the golfing and pool sketches, he has no opportunities to develop a characterization or to indulge in the leisurely creation of comic sequences. Thus, while in no sense illustrating a personal decline, "The

Big Broadcast of 1938" is a sorry swan song to an extraordinarily productive twelve-year association between Fields and Paramount.

Following his temporary withdrawal from films, Fields devoted himself to rebuilding his health and to a new—and what he thought would be an easier—career in radio. Despite having less leeway in meticulously timed radio material, and having to be cunningly cajoled into speeding up his delivery, Fields was an instant success. His dry humor could work without visual aids, and audiences delighted in his deliberate baiting of his sponsor's product (Chase and Sanborn Coffee) and his unsubtle slams at other important radio performers. As always, Fields tended to disregard scripts, wrote in his own material, and ad-libbed outrageously. Fortunately his co-star, ventriloquist Edgar Bergen, possessed a sharp wit and was able to convert potential disaster into what appeared to be well-organized repartee. A running gag was developed from a feud between Fields and Bergen's principal dummy, Charlie McCarthy, and this led to a return to films.

But before that took place it seemed that Fields might be out of movies permanently. Screen comedy in the thirties had undergone a number of changes, especially since the Production Code "reforms" in 1933, and Fields' misogynistic and generally anti-social conduct was now less attuned than ever to what executives supposed to be the public taste. Paramount, which had conformed to these regulations as readily as any other studio, had shown remarkable forbearance in not trying to reshape Fields according to the new standards. Oddly enough, elements of his screen character were even then being used by the English comic, Will Hay. It would be enormously unfair to accuse Hay, a distinguished comedian in his own right, of deliberately imitating Fields. British screen comedy enjoyed its richest period in the thirties, when the prolific number of regional comedians from the music halls, together with the national top-liners from radio and the London variety theatres, found a ready market for their talents in English films.

The comedy tradition in British silent films had never been strong, and, the sound films having no roots of their own to draw on other than the music halls, it was inevitable that the British studios would be strongly influenced by Hollywood comedies of the twenties, and, to a lesser degree, of the earlier thirties. Most of the principal Hollywood comedians—Laurel and Hardy, Harry Langdon, Harold Lloyd, Charlie Chase—were recognizable American types, types that have their counterparts in most countries. (Stan Laurel was English, of course, but accepted as American.)

The prodigious number of comics at work in British comedy films of the thirties also included many national prototypes who resembled their opposite numbers in Hollywood. Thus Harry Langdon was in a sense reincarnated in Lancashire comedian George Formby, and Jack Hulbert played the self-confident yet simple young go-getter exemplified by Harold Lloyd. Formby, like Langdon, was a perpetual innocent, and escaping from the seductive wiles of vampish villainesses was a problem common to them. Hulbert, like Lloyd, combined action

Fields, in "The Big Broadcast of 1938." (Courtesy of Paramount Pictures)

and thrills with his comedy. The Marx Brothers found a rough approximation in The Crazy Gang.

Will Hay, who became the most popular British screen comedian of the thirties, came from the music halls; his best known characterization was that of an inefficient schoolmaster who, with bluster and bombast, ruled large schoolboys who knew far more than he did—a routine he used, with variations, in several movies. Hay wrote much of his own material and was a competent director, but he never caught on as a solo performer. He needed to work with a team, and he found ideal compatriots who were neither straight men nor stooges in Graham Moffatt, a rotund youth whose ideas were usually sound, and Moore Marriott, playing a toothless octogenarian whose nuisance value occasionally gave way to rare moments of inspiration. The three were united in being harmlessly corrupt, mildly dishonest and totally inefficient except at small-time chicanery and avoiding honest toil. (They were usually employed in such civic pursuits as policemen, firemen or railwaymen.)

Like Fields, Hay was a braggart and a blusterer, frequently trapped by his

John Barrymore, also nearing the end of his Paramount contract, clowns with Fields—one of his closest friends—for a publicity still. (Courtesy of Paramount Pictures)

own schemings. But while Fields could bluff his way out of any situation by convincingly assuming the pose of an expert, Hay's attempts at bluff merely got him into more trouble. Hay used an ill-fitting pince-nez as a visual symbol of former dignity, just as Fields used a battered top hat; the pompous bray that Fields brought into play as his sign of authority was paralleled in Hay with a nasal sniff that could express condescension, disbelief or scorn. In many respects, Hay was a far more unlikeable character than Fields, with fewer redeeming traits. He was never a family man, so was denied the warmth and sympathy that Fields usually gained as a loving father or a henpecked husband. And when Hay came out on top— usually by capturing smugglers, the British equivalent of the cattle-rustler as the standard movie heavy—it was invariably not through altruistic motives, but through the purely selfish ones of trying to cover up his own mistakes or misdeeds.

The satisfaction in Fields films came from watching him stumble through to riches and happiness that, if not undeserved, were usually unearned. The satisfaction in Hay films was in seeing all of his plans come to naught; even in the nominally happy endings there were usually last-minute wrap-up gags which successfully robbed Hay of his temporary triumph. Interestingly enough, while the Hay character very much trod into Fieldsian territory, his plots and sight gags seemed equally influenced by Keaton. "Windbag the Sailor" is a fairly careful reworking of the basic structure and gags of Keaton's "The Navigator," and Hay's best film—1937's "Oh Mr. Porter!" with a prolonged train chase as its climax—owes a great deal to "The General." To further compound the international flavor of the Hay films, the best of them were directed not by Englishmen, but by the French Marcel Varnel and the American William Beaudine. Hay's films stand the test of time very well and are uniquely British enough not to appear to be mere lazy imitations of Fields or Keaton. They were not widely shown in the United States however; the rapid patter and the three contrasting dialects employed by Hay, Moffatt and Marriott would have made them largely incomprehensible to American audiences. Most were not released here at all.

Whether Fields ever saw any of the Hay films we cannot know; probably not, for he was suspicious of all competing comics, and the notion that any of them even indirectly purloined his material would have been sufficient to bring on lawsuits and convulsions. A story is told that he was taken to see a revival of Chaplin's "Easy Street" in the early forties, and left in the middle muttering sourly to himself that Chaplin was "a goddam ballet dancer" whom he would like "to strangle with my bare hands."

The chances of Fields' being introduced to Chaplin's work that late seem remote, yet one can understand Fields' reaction to Chaplin and can believe in the remark even if Fields said it many years before.

Fields, in the early days, ranked far below Chaplin, and he undoubtedly sensed that Chaplin got laughs from an aggression and mild sadism quite akin to his own, yet masked with a grace—and sentimentality—that Fields could never match, even if he had wanted to. He might have been less incensed at Will Hay; Hay borrowed openly from Fields style but never gained the same audience empathy and reaped fewer dividends.

If Fields had seen Hay and been annoyed by him, in all probability he would have settled scores his own way by adding a rascally thief of a British schoolteacher to his rogues' gallery of tent-show impresarios, bank presidents and absconding tellers! Although Hay made no silents, his talkie career roughly paralleled that of Fields. He made his last film in the early forties while in poor health, and he died not long afterward.

Fields faces severest threat since Baby LeRoy. With Edgar Bergen and Charlie McCarthy; "You Can't Cheat an Honest Man." (Courtesy of Universal Pictures)

☞ 14.

The Move to Universal

The success of the Fields-Edgar Bergen radio shows and the improvement in Fields' health inevitably suggested his return to the movies with Bergen as a team-mate, and the proposal was put forward by Universal Pictures.

Universal were weak on comedy names at that time, although a year or so later they would add the Ritz Brothers to their roster and develop the new team of Abbott and Costello. Edgar Bergen, with Charlie McCarthy, had already scored a resounding hit at Universal in "A Letter of Introduction," a good if somewhat old-fashioned emotional drama in which their comedy relief all but stole the show.

Fields was to be very much the star of the new film and indeed wrote the story under his pseudonym of Charles Bogle, giving it the title "You Can't Cheat an Honest Man," to the eternal bafflement of the front office. Nevertheless, while it was to be designed as a Fields vehicle, Universal probably were counting on the popularity of Bergen and the novelty of his ventriloquist act to put the film over. Commercially, they may have been right. The film attracted swarms of younger film fans to whom Fields was but a name from the dim past and for

Fields, as ventriloquist and charlatan-at-large, in "You Can't Cheat an Honest Man." (Courtesy of Universal Pictures)

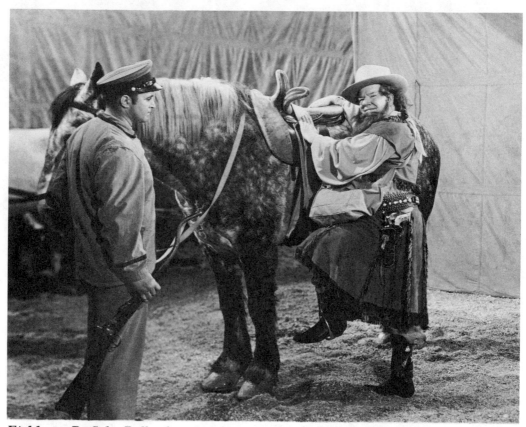

Fields as Buffalo Bella, bearded lady circus star; "You Can't Cheat an Honest Man." (Courtesy of Universal Pictures)

whom Bergen and his dolls were the main attraction. To them, the Fields interludes were but tedious interruptions to the Bergen material.

Today, while Bergen's personality remains pleasing, and the dummies—hayseed Mortimer Snerd, even more than city slicker Charlie McCarthy—are ingenious and have real personalities, it is the mechanical and dated ventriloquist interludes which now seem to be injected arbitrarily.

There were difficulties from the first. George Marshall, assigned to direct, was an experienced comedy man who had worked with Laurel and Hardy, among others, but who was a versatile all-round director. He worked quickly and efficiently and stood no nonsense from anyone, hence there was bound to be trouble with Fields, to whom scripts (even his own) meant nothing and shooting schedules even less. The official assistant director was Vernon Keays, regularly a director of "B" westerns, and his function was largely that of a second-unit man, staging and shooting the stunt action scenes and the climactic chase.

To relieve friction and to keep production rolling, a third director was brought in, Eddie Cline, who had worked with Fields only once before, on "Mil-

In the shower; "You Can't Cheat an Honest Man." (Courtesy of Universal Pictures)

lion Dollar Legs." For reasons never sufficiently explained, Fields took a sadistic delight in baiting Cline, in mocking all of his suggestions, and generally in conveying the impression that he was the incompetent of all time.

Yet somehow the film was shot—Cline working with Fields, Marshall with Bergen, his dummies and the romantic interest (Constance Moore). And somewhere along the way Fields must have come to realize that he was in the wrong, for he evidently made his peace with Cline. The next three Fields vehicles at Universal were all directed by Cline—something that Fields would never have stood for had serious disagreements continued—and the overall quality of those films, combining Fields' material with the slick production efficiency so typical of Cline, indicates that a comfortable working rapport must have been established.

"You Can't Cheat an Honest Man" was atypical in one major sense. For once, Fields—playing Larson E. Whipsnade, circus impresario—was an almost total scoundrel, an unrepentant chiseler forever on the run from the law, and so insensitive to his daughter's happiness that he tries to force her into a marriage for money.

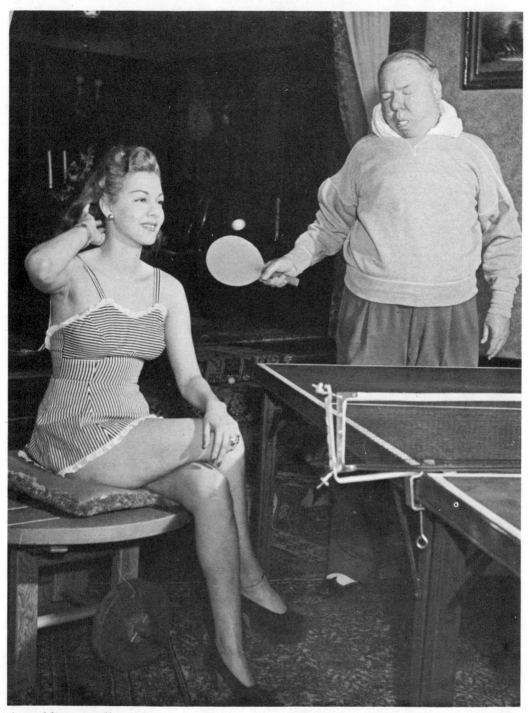

A publicity still of Fields practicing his table-tennis routine for "You Can't Cheat an Honest Man" with starlet Maria Montez paying more attention to the camera than to him. (Courtesy of Universal Pictures)

Behind these portals most of the unlikely plot elements in "The Bank Dick" take shape. (Courtesy of Universal Pictures)

The eventual happy ending is brought about not so much by Fields' undergoing a change of heart as the fact that his daughter, herself disgusted by the snobbery of the wealthy family into which she is marrying, calls it off. There is a vicious quality to this new Fields which may well have been a hangover from the tongue-lashing he engaged in so freely in his radio scripts.

In 1939 he could still get away with his half-friendly racial slurs (directed mainly at Eddie "Rochester" Anderson and other indolent crap-shooting colored handymen in "You Can't Cheat an Honest Man") and his frequent "Godfrey Daniels!" In other ways, many of his gags were affected by the more cautious methods of the late thirties.

One of the most amusing sight gags in the picture shows him taking a shower behind a circus tent. Queenie the elephant sprays him with water, and, his toilet finished, he covers his nakedness to some extent by replacing his sporty bowler hat. Then he strolls nonchalantly through the fairgrounds, the camera following him in a long tracking shot, with various obstructions—a folded sheet, a crate, a wagon—discreetly coming between him and camera and shielding his nether regions from view.

Suddenly, from the rear of the screen, and approaching Fields from his unprotected side, appears a prim little spinster. She spies the pink and freshly scrubbed Fields body and lets out a shriek of outrage and horror. Belligerently Fields glowers at her as she turns tail and runs for safety. Then he moves out from behind the final obstruction to reveal that he *is* wearing trousers after all. The audience has had its belly-laugh, but the point has been immediately nullified by this sell-out.

A similar joke in Laurel and Hardy's "Putting Pants on Philip" of 1927 does not cheat in this way, and not only does the audience continue laughing in happy recollection for the next several minutes, but variations on the gag can be worked for the rest of the film. The feeling of having been "had" brings this big laugh to an instant grinding halt in "You Can't Cheat an Honest Man," and it is several minutes before the damage can be repaired.

At various points in the film Fields stations himself in the box office to sell tickets, and uses this as a vantage point from which to rattle off his favorite gags. He complains of "kids reeking of popcorn," and is bilked of a dollar by a freckle-faced brat who bawls out a lying story about the circus elephant just having trampled her dog to death. Bells clang continuously, the wooden flap on the box-office window falls with a resounding crunch on his fingers, an assistant apears too interested in his bottle—"Keep your hands off my lunch"—he gets his foot jammed in a bucket, falls through the floor boards, is harried by an angry pup, and all the while continues selling tickets with a barrage of repartee and insults directed at his paying customers.

When a lawman comes along to inquire if he is Larson E. Whipsnade he hurriedly stuffs a piece of rope under his nose to simulate a Teutonic moustache, and adopts a wickedly exaggerated stereotyped German accent. When he gets involved with an angry woman who complains that he has fleeced her, he sur-reptitiously knocks her down and then, for the benefit of a gathering crowd, com-mends the stricken woman to her husband, telling her, "Make him drag you home—he got you drunk!" While frequently losing his hat on his cane, he rat-tles off such brisk one-liners as "Some weasel took the cork out of my lunch!" and—an instruction to the elephant who is providing his shower-bath—"Hold it longer—heat it up a bit!"

The Bergen-McCarthy-Fields altercations are relatively few in "You Can't Cheat an Honest Man." For the most part Bergen works his routines alone with the dummies, or with the charming and graceful Constance Moore, who, as Fields' daughter, is used as a link between the two stars. There is one good and amusingly written sequence in which Fields tries to "assassinate" McCarthy, and Bergen traces him through the various wild animal cages, finally rescuing Charlie alive from the stomach of a crocodile!

Fields at one point stages a mock ventriloquist act himself, wearing a false moustache with repulsive artificial teeth attached. His ring-master braggadocio includes a gem where he introduces two perfectly ordinary performers with the build-up: "Two brothers who baffle science—side by side, the world's smallest giant and the world's largest midget!"

Later, wearing thick black whiskers while unconvincingly attired in a span-gled cow-girl outfit, and brandishing a gun with a barrel as crooked as his old "warped" golf club, he bounces around on a huge wreck of a horse, billing himself as "Buffalo Bella, the bearded lady sharpshooter, riding the largest Shetland pony in the world!" As he dismounts from this particular display he is accosted by yet another sheriff, but once more he is too smart for the law. "I'm Gertrude Schickle-gruber," he announces coyly, raising his fist to ward off an expected attack, and los-ing his whiskers in the process.

Fields' best material is held for the final reel, when he holds sway quite alone on the screen. Bergen, McCarthy and Mortimer Snerd have been dis-posed of, Fields having set them adrift in a balloon; they crash-land, run into Fields' daughter on the way to her engagement party at the Bel Goodies, and all four of them wind up in jail. This leaves Fields to tackle the Bel Goodies alone, and he arrives at their mansion in fine style, driven in a circus chariot by one of his colored hands at whom he hurls a snarled "I hate you!" for reckless driving, before sauntering into the snooty society home and carefully laying out his cape where the free advertising imprinted on it will be seen to its best advantage.

All of Hollywood's stuffed-shirts, from perennial society matron Mary Forbes to eternal gigolo Ivan Lebedeff, are at the party, and picking it up where the similar party in "Her Majesty Love" left off, Fields soon has the upper-crust crumbling. "Lots of necks washed here tonight," he beams amiably, and to his no-good weakling son Phineas (who seems to have no logical reason for being in the film at all), he mutters in an aside, "All of the creme-de-la-creme is here to-night . . . they have noblesse oblige . . . we have acrobats." Mrs. Bel Goodie tries to quiet this awful man, and asks him what is keeping his daughter. "She's gone to a barber shop for a facial . . . she may be some time . . . there were eight or nine men ahead of her."

Somehow this reminds him of a story that has to do with snakes, but at the mention of the word "snake" Mrs. Bel Goodie screams and collapses in a faint. Mr. Bel Goodie, harassed and perspiring, played by that superb society blusterer Thurston Hall, takes Fields aside and tells him that Mrs. Bel Goodie suffers from an odd malady—so strong an aversion to snakes that she faints even at the mention of them. "How unfortunate," murmurs Fields distantly, listening at the same time to another guest's inquiry after the prostrate Mrs. Bel Goodie, and informing him that she's had too much to drink. Mrs. Bel Goodie valiantly rouses herself, determined to carry on, but she regains her senses just as Fields lunges into the protracted and unlikely history of a snake's astonishing devotion to a human who had befriended him—a devotion so deep and so profound that when his benefactor was attacked, the snake rushed to his defense, sinking his fangs into the marauder's fetlocks.

The tale, told slowly and deliberately and with repeated emphasis on the word "snake," is punctuated by periodic screams from the now thoroughly shattered Mrs. Bel Goodie. At the end of his recital, Fields is persuaded to change the subject. Hurt that his efforts to entertain are not fully appreciated, Fields suggests that he might make amends by telling that yarn about the drummer. "No, no!" protests son Phineas, seeing the Bel Goodie fortune flying out of the window. "You'll ruin everything." "I could clean it up a bit," suggests Fields cajolingly.

Fortunately the situation is saved when a hardy society matron asks him "How is your ping pong?" With a look that says he regards her question as an obscene impertinence he replies scathingly, "Fine, how's yours?"

Bats and ball are produced, and the game is on, a slam-bang, no-holds-barred match that moves from ante-room to dining room, out to the patio—where the ping-pong ball is temporarily detoured into a fountain—and back again. A mighty swipe from Fields' bat sends the ping-pong ball squarely into a society matron's open mouth, but another vigorous swat, applied to the back of her neck, launches the ball back into play again. Splendidly edited, and with Fields showing inimitable grace and skill as he bats the ball back and forth in a number of long uninterrupted takes, the game brings to a fitting climax one of the funniest of all Fields sequences.

His daughter arrives just in time to hear the Bel Goodies giving him a thorough dressing-down. Son Phineas improbably regains his integrity and, together with his sister, informs the Bel Goodies that they want no part of their family. With an elegant hat-twiddle, Fields tells Mr. Bel Goodie that he is nothing less than a Tartuffle, and leaves with as much solemnity as he can muster. His dignity is short-lived, however; the sheriff is on his trail once more, and the circus caravan makes a helter-skelter dash for the state line, reaching safety with moments to spare. The Whipsnade financial problems remain unsolved, but at

Each star had his own director in "You Can't Cheat an Honest Man."
(Above) W. C. Fields with Eddie Cline. (Courtesy of Universal Pictures) (Below)
Edgar Bergen (and Charlie McCarthy) with George Marshall. (Courtesy of Univer-
sal Pictures)

Constance Moore was Fields' daughter in "You Can't Cheat an Honest Man."
(Courtesy of Universal Pictures)

Having frightened his hostess (Mary Forbes) into a dead faint and outraged his host (Thurston Hall), Fields contemplates next move; "You Can't Cheat an Honest Man." (Courtesy of Universal Pictures)

least for the moment there is a breathing spell, and the undesirability of the Bel Goodies as close kin seems to have reconciled Whipsnade to having the penni-less Bergen as a son-in-law.

Despite its flaws, "You Can't Cheat an Honest Man" was a good movie, well-paced, better mounted in terms of production values and of mobility and variety of camera-work than most Fields vehicles, and above all, the funniest comedy he had made since "The Man on the Flying Trapeze" in 1935. His comeback was off to an auspicious start.

W. C. *(Cuthbert J. Twillie) Fields awaits train on private railroad platform; "My Little Chickadee."* (Courtesy of Universal Pictures)

Fields Tames the West

For three years, Universal Pictures had been having serious problems. Until 1936, under the old Carl Laemmle regime, they had been riding high as one of the less affluent but nevertheless reliable major companies. They turned out a goodly portion of "bread and butter" product, but they also made the best and most stylish horror films; genuine "prestige" items such as "The Kiss Before the Mirror" and "Once More River"; epics like "Sutter's Gold," and occasional box-office blockbusters of the stature of "Show Boat."

Their directors had included some of the best and most talented in the business—James Whale, John Ford, James Cruze, Frank Borzage, Gregory La Cava. Then, suddenly, the bottom dropped out. Faced with serious losses, the whole company was reorganized, its production policy changed, and even the company title changed to New Universal, a globe revolving in a glittering, star-filled sky replacing the simpler and more dramatic trademark of the biplane circling the world.

The aim now was at economy and "family" entertainment, and that aim was clearly illustrated by the immediate change in product. The virile old Buck Jones westerns—as popular with adults as with juveniles—were replaced by the slick but rather pedestrian musical westerns with Bob Baker. The grim and stylish Karloff and Lugosi horror films were ushered out just as Universal's newest and biggest star, Deanna Durbin, was ushered in. Almost overnight, Universal's average schedule of forty-five films a year became primarily "B" pictures, with a few economical "A"s thrown in.

Despite the glittering new trademark, the star roster was singularly unimpressive. Durbin was the only really big name they had, with respectable (but not major) names like Douglas Fairbanks, Jr., and Danielle Darrieux brought in for odd one-shot pictures. 1937 and 1938 were years of retrenchment; in 1939 Universal felt ready to re-establish itself as a major company again. Bigger productions (albeit with a shrewd eye on all possible economies) were scheduled, and an all-out drive was started to bring star names into the fold again, either for single pictures or on a contractual basis. The aim seemed to be to acquire stars who still had name and prestige value but who had slipped sufficiently so that their asking prices would not be exorbitant. On this basis, Bing Crosby, Charles Boyer, Irene Dunne, Basil Rathbone, Douglas Fairbanks, Jr., George Raft, Victor McLaglen, James Stewart and Marlene Dietrich were acquired to lend some solid support to Miss Durbin's earning capacities.

As if to acknowledge that their older ideas of what the public wanted might have been right after all, Karloff and Lugosi were brought back to start off a whole new horror cycle with "Son of Frankenstein," and with Johnny Mack Brown as their new western star, Universal's outdoor epics returned to the more rugged level of earlier days too.

It was under this set-up that both W. C. Fields and Mae West came to Universal. Both had been big Paramount stars in the earlier thirties—too big ever to appear together—and both had been slipping at the box office, their pictures becoming more and more infrequent. Mae West especially had suffered from the increasingly stringent restrictions placed on her scripts by the Production Code. Since a change of studio wouldn't alter the Hays Office facts of life, the idea of co-starring her with Fields seemed a sound one. Worried about Fields' appeal, Universal had given him Edgar Bergen and Charlie MacCarthy for his first Universal film, earlier that same year.

The strategy had worked with "You Can't Cheat an Honest Man," and it should work again with "My Little Chickadee." Mae West, with Fields to back her up, wouldn't have to rely entirely on her own bag of tricks to see her through, and comedy weaknesses in her pictures caused by compromise with the Production Code could be overcome by substituting less censorable Fieldsian material. Although the strategy did work, it suceeded principally because of the Fields presence. The whole film could have worked purely as a western spoof starring Fields solo; but it could only have been a limp echo of Mae West's earlier "Goin' to Town"—a semi-western—had it been attempted as a solo vehicle for her.

Twillie acknowledges greetings of train engineer; "My Little Chickadee." (Courtesy of Universal Pictures)

"Destry Rides Again," made that same year by the same studio, provided a formidable comeback vehicle for Marlene Dietrich and launched her on a whole new career, but "My Little Chickadee" worked no such wonders for Mae West. Her era was over, just as Clara Bow's had been over when the twenties faded into the thirties. "My Little Chickadee" would have been a fine swan song for Mae West had she not decided to make one more unfortunate comeback attempt in the early forties.

As was usual with both of them, Mae West and Fields insisted on writing their own stories, and the collaboration proved to be a smooth one. Miss West's method was to travel in a straight line, regardless of logic, and to spoof clichés deliberately, so that when she wanted to use them seriously they served the purpose of carrying the plot forward, the audience being unaware that on this occasion no satire was intended. Fields, on the other hand, cared little for plot. He was only concerned with setting up individual gags and routines and filling them with vaudevillian characters and fall-guys. Since Mae West rarely used interesting supporting players, preferring to use actors who would be merely

175

straight men for her, Fields' inventive zeal in this area helped enliven "My Little Chickadee" a great deal.

Writing their own material, both performers seem to have been happy, and there was a surprising lack of friction between them while shooting the film. Indeed, Fields seemed far more worried that he might one day bump into Deanna Durbin, whom he professed to detest because she had moved into a house next to his. Alarmed lest she might practice singing in her garden, he had announced that he kept a rifle by his open window, and would shoot to kill if necessary! The showdown never came, however, and within a couple of years Fields had mellowed sufficiently to appear in pictures with such second-string Durbins as Gloria Jean and Jane Powell.

Fields and Mae West worked well together, and if there were mutual suspicions about the other trying to swing the emphasis to his or her advantage, they didn't show in the harmonious performances that emerged on screen. A more demanding financial and business wizard than Fields, however, Miss West saw to it that she got first billing in the film's credits. Their names appeared together three times, twice as stars and once as writers, side by side and in letters scrupulously the same size, but with Miss West's name on the left of the screen, which is the preferred position even in equal billing.

While the two stars emerged with relatively equal footage, it was Fields who walked away with the show. His solo routines were hilarious, light on sight gags and with none of the great visual set-pieces of his old Paramount films, but strong on bar-room and card-game sequences which gave him full rein in nonsensical, rambling conversations and acid repartee. In his scenes with Mae West —and while they appear together throughout the film, there are only two or three sequences in which they really work together as a team—he is the dominating figure, with Miss West being reduced to little more than playing straight for him, a position which had been filled for her by Cary Grant, Paul Cavanagh, Randolph Scott and other leading men.

Fields makes no obvious attempts to steal scenes by the ordinary methods of mugging, or distracting byplay with props; he seems cunningly aware of Mae West's own self-confidence, and of the fact that her innuendoes and eye-flutterings will no longer get the audience response that she has learned to expect. He is content to rely on the droll delivery of his lines to win the scenes for him, and his judgment is sound. Miss West's solo sequences, though well-written and amusing, seem forced and dated. When she is alone, it becomes obvious that she is of necessity pulling her punches. The sneers and hip-wigglings with which she punctuates her dialogue are not justified by the fairly mild content and lack of bite of the lines themselves, while the too measured editing, assuming bigger and longer laughs than were forthcoming, and leaving "dead" footage to accommodate them, slows down the pace of her solo scenes considerably.

Far better for the viewer to lose a line completely, as one frequently did in the old Paramount days, when her quips tumbled over one another so fast that the laughter never had time to subside, than to wait for gag lines, and in waiting have time to build up expectancies that are never quite fulfilled. Mae West's part in "My Little Chickadee" also suffers from a vaguely defined romance with a masked outlaw, so blurred by being kept within the confines of approved Production Code sexual behavior that it is never clearly established as being either burlesque or merely old-fashioned dramatics. Too obvious studio "exteriors" in these scenes are also distracting.

The first reel of "My Little Chickadee" is devoted exclusively to Mae West, establishing her as the semi-willing abduction victim of a masked stagecoach robber. The puritanical townspeople run her out of town, and take the precaution of telegraphing ahead to her next stop—Greasewood City—to advise the Ladies' Aid Society that the notorious Flowerbelle is en route. This whole sequence resembled one in John Ford's "Stagecoach," which opens with prostitute Claire Trevor being run out of town by militant ladies. (The Ford film was released shortly before "My Little Chickadee" went into production.)

The train bearing Mae West to Greasewood City comes to an unscheduled halt when a tired-looking Indian brave, a donkey and a snoozing Fields block the track. Rousing himself from his slumbers, Fields asks of the locomotive in general, "Do you have any private cars with a room and bath and exclusive bar?" The engineer shakes his head. "Drat!" mutters Fields imperiously, but gathers his belongings anyway and boards the train.

He is Cuthbert J. Twillie, and from his carpet-bag filled with bank-notes, it is obvious that he is not quite the city simpleton that his white flower buttonhole and over-sized stovepipe hat would indicate. Ambling through the coach, muttering pleasantries as he searches for a vacant seat opposite the most vulnerable-looking passenger, he stumbles over his umbrella, bending it completely out of shape.

"Don't worry, it can't break," he croons, straightening it out again, "it's a genuine Chamberlain!" (British audiences were noticeably cool to this reference to their umbrella-toting Prime Minister.) Twillie finds a seat next to that perennial movie gossip, Margaret Hamilton. Suddenly, Indians attack the train (an exciting sequence as well as an amusing one, elaborately staged and well photographed) and Flowerbelle takes charge, blazing away with two six-shooters and rapidly decimating the marauders. "There he goes in a shower of feathers," she murmurs as yet another Indian bites the dust.

Twillie's behavior is less heroic, his first retaliation being limited to snarling "I hate you!" at the Indian whose arrows whiz past his head. Attempting to escape into the next car, he finds himself momentarily in the open, grabs an arrow from mid-air as it flies past his ear, and flings it back at the Indians. Finding a relatively safe position, he lets fly at the attackers with a child's catapult. The boy from whom he has stolen it demands it back, but Twillie soon disposes of him, pushing him out into the enemy fire with the command: "Go in there and fight like a man!"

Fields displays his "genuine Chamberlain" umbrella to Margaret Hamilton;
"My Little Chickadee." (Courtesy of Universal Pictures)

Thanks to Flowerbelle's marksmanship the battle is soon over, a group of now riderless Indian ponies watching forlornly as the Iron Horse steams away. Bowled over by Flowerbelle—the only remotely pretty woman on the train—Twillie seeks more information. "Tell me about the lady with the hot-house cognomen," he asks of his traveling companion, and collecting all his belongings in a manner to give the lie to his murmured, "I'll be right back," he moves in on Flowerbelle, all courtesy and gallantry as he asks permission to kiss her "symmetrical digits." Flowerbelle attempts to brush him off quickly, and when he asks her to tell him something about herself, she says that she can't tell him anything good.

"I can see what's good," retorts Twillie; "tell me the rest."

The hatchet-face gossip tries to break it up with a verbal tirade, but fails. "I hope she doesn't get too violent," mutters Twillie. "I haven't strength enough to knock her down." Flowerbelle in the meantime has glimpsed the minor mountains of money in Twillie's bag, and changes her tactics. "It is not good for man to be alone," booms Twillie, and coyly she agrees: "It's no fun for a woman either." Overjoyed, Fields suggests, "Could we be lonesome together?"

178

With borrowed weapon, Fields fights off attacking redskins in "My Little Chicka-dee." (Courtesy of Universal Pictures)

Striking while the iron is hot, Miss West goes off to enlist the aid of Donald Meek, a card-sharp whose clothing and demeanor cause him to be mistaken for a minister. (Another casual lifting from "Stagecoach," in which Meek played a whiskey drummer invariably believed to be a minister.)

A phoney wedding is accomplished, despite the minister's occasional lapses into the vernacular of the card-sharp ("All right, I'll deal," he remarks as the happy couple stand before him); the train arrives at Greasewood City and the newlyweds head for the hotel. Twillie is mildly surprised when his bride books two rooms, and decidedly perplexed when the nuptial chamber door is slammed in his face. Rasping his old complaint about the Ethiopian in the fuel supply, he adds rather sorrowfully, "Evidently I'm getting the old heave-ho." Helpfully, a hotel clerk informs him that his room is just down the hall. "Leave it there, I'll find it," grumbles Twillie, as possibilities of marital bliss fade.

Yet there is always the chance that his bride is merely suffering from wedding night jitters. "Egad, the child's afraid of me . . . she's all a'twit," he rumbles to no one in particular, then bends down to bellow through the keyhole, "I have

179

certain very definite pear-shaped ideas to discuss with you." Flowerbelle opens the door with unexpected suddenness, catapulting Fields into a spectacular prat-fall. Fields was fond of the violent fall—over a chair, down a flight of stairs, through a trapdoor—as a piece of regular comedy punctuation. He uses three or four such falls in "My Little Chickadee," always with stunt doubles.

Mae West makes it plain that marital pleasures must be postponed, and Fields wanders disconsolately downstairs where his faithful Indian retainer is wait-ing to greet him with the question, "New squaw?"

"New is right," answers the disgruntled Twillie. "She hasn't even been un-wrapped yet." Upstairs, Flowerbelle, to the inappropriate background music of the Zampa Overture, is going through her husband's belongings and discovers that the wealth of paper money is in reality a vast collection of coupons redeem-able against Twillie's elixirs and other sucker products.

Twillie meanwhile retires to the more familiar terrain of the local saloon. The bartender (Jimmy Conlin) turns out to be an old friend, and they swap reminiscences. The big poker game in progress is too rich for Twillie's blood, but he finds a lone gambler who somewhat suspiciously agrees to a sporting wager to see who can cut the highest card. He puts his hundred dollars on the table, and Twillie camouflages his inability to match it with a flowery little speech. "I'm traveling light—the country is fraught with marauders. I'll give you my personal I.O.U. (a pause here for effect and a confidential glance), something I seldom give to strangers!" The gambler cuts the cards and comes up with a king. "Oh, tut tut," smiles Twillie ingratiatingly.

"Don't show me the card, a gentleman's game!"

Twillie makes his cut, looks at his card, hurriedly replaces it in the pack, and calmly remarks, "Ace," as he reaches for his winnings. The gambler, dubious, but inclined to disbelieve that anyone would try such a brazen bluff, protests that he hasn't seen the card. "Oh very well," grumbles Twillie in mild irritation, and thumbs through the pack until he finds the ace. "There it is, if you must satisfy your morbid curiosity."

Twillie mistakes the gambler's impotent rage for acquiescence, and with a false, comradely smile, suggests, "Shall we have another go at it?" A closer study of his opponent's face tells him that retreat might be the wiser tactic at this mo-ment. "No? Perhaps at some future date."

Twillie ambles off with his hundred-dollar winning to the big game, seats himself amid the cigar smoke and piles of gambling chips, and grandiosely de-mands one hundred dollars' worth of chips. The dealer contemptuously hands him one chip, and in an effort to regain stature, Twillie launches into an ac-count of an expedition into the wilds of Afghanistan. "We lost our corkscrew and were compelled to live on food and water for several days," he concludes rather lamely as the gamblers holler at him to shut up and play cards.

Before long, Twillie's cheating is recognized, and he is about to be man-handled by the mob. Vainly he argues that he is a stranger and unfamiliar with

Donald Meek, W. C. Fields, Mae West. Three master con-artists meet; "My Little Chickadee." (Courtesy of Universal Pictures)

the rules; is there a book he can purchase, so that this unfortunate accident will not happen again? Luckily Flowerbelle's arrival prevents serious mayhem; she has found favor with the saloon owner, Joseph Calleia (who also happens to be the masked bandit who abducted her).

For the time being Twillie is saved, and he goes off murmuring and clucking about his shock at being accused of chicanery. Soon he has completely recovered his aplomb and is regaling the saloon habitués with stories of how he slaughtered the savages who attacked the train. In his enthusiasm, he describes firing three six-shooters all at once. In response to an innocent inquiry as to how this could be done, he demonstrates—Bang! Bang! And then there is a teeth-grinding spit as he pulls the third trigger with his tongue! Admirers shake his hand in adulation, and he grimaces slightly: "Watch that trigger finger!"

The saloon crowd isn't eager to accommodate Twillie in any more poker games, however, and we next see him playing cards with his Indian servant. "Three squaws!" exclaims the Indian triumphantly, but is topped by Twillie with "Three chiefs!" The Indian moves to pick up his bow and arrow, and Twillie growls sus-

Play 'em close to the vest—and chins—especially when out of chips; "My Little Chickadee." (Courtesy of Universal Pictures)

Caught cheating, Twillie begs to know where he can "purchase a book of rules." *"My Little Chickadee."* (Courtesy of Universal Pictures)

piciously, "What are you up to, you red rascal?"—slugging him with a bottle before he has a chance to answer.

"All they can get me for is splitting a bottle of whiskey with an Indian," he grins complacently.

His next victim is Flowerbelle's cousin, played by Fuzzy Knight, a yokel who has come to see how his relative is settling down to married life. Getting rid of his Indian shadow—"Go back to the reservation and milk your elk!"—Twillie butters up his new victim with some Fieldsian soft soap and easily gets him into a card game. "Is this a game of chance?" innocently inquires Cousin Zeb. "Not the way I play it, no," replies Twillie as the scene fades.

From this point on, Mae West has lost control of the film; a raucous song number and a lively sequence in which she takes over as a schoolteacher fail to wrest dominance back from Fields. (Stills are an unreliable guide, many being shot purely for publicity purposes, but it would appear that even more Fields material than we see in the picture was shot and later deleted. Stills show him in a burlesque western costume that he does not wear in the film, driving a stagecoach and riding an old high-wheeled bicycle.)

Twillie has succeeded in becoming elected sheriff, a position he accepts proudly, unaware that the mortality rate among law officers in Greasewood City is staggeringly high. At a banquet in the new sheriff's honor, the crooked saloon owner extols Twillie's virtues while the camera slowly tracks the length of the table to find the guest of honor at the foot, sitting half inside an open closet door. Coat sleeves and a dainty parasol that fall on him are soon disposed of, but a huge feather wrap is more of a problem. The feathers find their way into his soup, and almost into his stomach. Spluttering them out, he spears the offending wrap to the wall with a fork, and proceeds to enjoy his meal.

Fortune indeed seems to be smiling on Twillie this night; Flowerbelle indicates that from now on his husband-in-name-only status will be changed. In the boudoir, Twillie preens himself and announces that he will dip his pink and white body in the tub. "For the nonce, adieu!" he booms grandly. Flowerbelle reminds him to take his gloves off, and he vanishes into the bathroom, only to trip and fall into the empty tub.

While soaking in the tub, he keeps up a steady stream of loathsome small-talk, hoping to entertain his bride. He tells her of the time he caught malaria in the old swimming hole. "What a foul summer that was . . . the year the Jones boys murdered their mother . . . I can see her now. . . ." But Flowerbelle is not listening; her seductiveness is only a ruse to provide an alibi while she slips off to answer a summons from her masked lover. She hides a goat in the marital bed with the instructions, "Keep your mouth closed and let him do all the talking. . . . Do this right and I'll get you his straw hat!"

Twillie, who discovers too late that he forgot to take off his white kid gloves while bathing, finishes his toilet and attires himself elegantly in a frilly nightgown,

Fields luxuriating in bath before joining bride, Mae West, in "My Little Chickadee." For reasons unknown, his head has been taken from another photograph and pasted in here. (Courtesy of Universal Pictures)

his sheriff's badge pinned to the bodice. His flights of poetry provoking no response from his apparently sleeping bride, he reaches under the covers to caress her, and comes in contact with the goat's skin.

"You'd better take your coat off, dear," he tells her with a note of hope in his voice. "You won't feel the good of it when you go out." A closer embrace prompts him to add, "It smells like it hasn't been taken to the cleaners recently." The goat, its slumbers disturbed, moves to the side of the bed with a bleat. "Mama . . . she's calling for her mama . . . what sublime innocence," croons the happy bridegroom. But the goat has had enough, and scrambles out of bed, to the accompaniment of an enraged "Godfrey Daniel!" from Twillie.

Later that night, some of the townspeople pound on his door to inform him that there has been yet another stage hold-up. "How unfortunate," mutters Twillie, completely uninterested, though he agrees to the formation of a posse. "Posse by all means," he proclaims with determination, and then goes back to bed. "Sleep—the most beautiful experience in life—except drink!"

The sequence that follows, totally irrelevant to the plot, finds the sheriff tem-

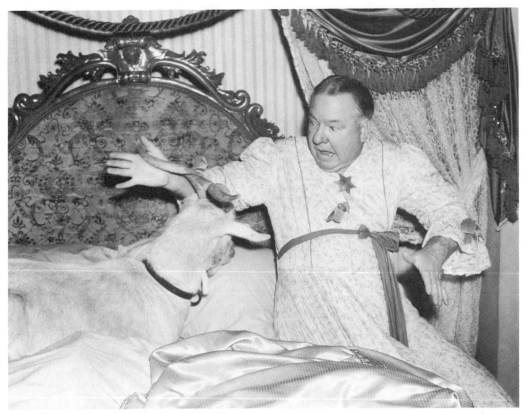

"Godfrey Daniel!" One of Fields' favorite movie cuss-words, uttered at finding goat in his bridal bed, instead of Mae West; "My Little Chickadee." (Courtesy of Universal Pictures)

porarily filling in as a bartender, and is one of the funniest bits of verbal by-play that Fields ever conceived. He and his old pal Jimmy Conlin again are swapping reminiscences as they tend bar. An aggressive lady customer enters and goes to the far end of the bar. Fields wanders up to serve her, casually walking over another minor barkeep in passing. A bar, or a store-counter—as in "The Pharmacist"—was a simple but cunning set that Fields used frequently. A camera, mounted on a dolly, could move along parallel with him, stop for closeups while he delivered specific chunks of dialogue, and then continue to move back and forth with him, bringing pace and movement to what otherwise might have been a stagey conversational interlude.

The aggressive lady is drunk, and Fields tries in vain to persuade her to go home. She wants only to unburden herself of her problems and tell Fields about her no-good husband. Fields nods sympathetically as she talks. "Oh, you're too quick-witted for him . . . too quick at repartee."

There is a momentary respite when another customer comes in to commiserate with Fields over a past tragedy that the script has thus far given no hint of.

"I hear you buried your wife," the new arrival remarks. "Yes, I had to," explains Fields. "She died."

The lady drunk staggers out. Fields heaves a sigh of relief, but when another customer remarks that she was a real tough egg, he demurs. "Tough nothing. If I had Squawk Mulligan with me and was in condition, I could lick two of 'em!" This reminds him of another tale, which he proceeds to tell with relish. It is the saga of one Chicago Nellie, and to give the tale its proper documentary flavor, Twillie first elaborates on the goodies available at the free-lunch counter in the saloon where the historic encounter occurred.

"It consisted of Philadelphia cream cheese, asparagus with mayonnaise. . . ." He describes the other gooey ingredients gleefully. ". . . And then Chicago Nellie dips her mitt into this *mélange*. . . ." In describing the fight that followed, Twillie takes altogether too much credit for being the hero of the fracas, and his claim that he jumped over the bar and knocked her down is fervently disputed by the other bartender.

"*I* knocked her down!" he insists. "All right," agrees Twillie reluctantly, "but I started kicking her." This unlooses another train of recollection. "Did you ever kick a woman in the midriff when she had corsets on?" Twillie asks his listener. The man thinks for a moment; "No, offhand I just can't recall any such incident." Twillie winces with pain at the memory. "It broke my toe." But the bottom falls out of his recounting of this titanic battle when the other bartender adds: "Later on she came back and beat up the both of us!" Twillie insists, however, in justification to himself, that all the facts be known.

"Yes, she did," he admits. "But she brought another woman with her. Elderly little woman, with grey hair. . . ."

His tale told, Twillie closes up the bar and leaves, recoiling from the sweet smile and proffered collection tambourine of a pretty Salvation Army girl waiting outside the saloon. He raises his hand to strike, thinks better of it, and goes back to the sheriff's office. There, a serious game of checkers is in progress. Twillie watches intently, sizing up the game thoroughly, anxious to help. "I wonder what would happen if . . ." he suggests, pointing out a particularly cunning move. The move is made, and the opponent promptly sweeps his rival off the board. Fields is mildly chagrined: "Oh, I see; well, just an experiment, that's all."

Irked by constant tales of Flowerbelle's *grande affaire* with the masked bandit, Twillie decides that the only way he will ever gain entrance to his wife's boudoir is by masquerading as the bandit himself. Noisily removing moth balls from an old suit and nuts from a black bag, he crunches back and forth over them as he fashions himself a bandit outfit. None too agilely scaling a ladder, he finds himself in Flowerbelle's room and almost immediately the recipient of passionate kisses. But the quality of Twillie's kisses, and the tell-tale nose protruding through the mask, quickly give the game away. Twillie is unabashed, however, when Flowerbelle calls him a cheat.

Identified as masked bandit, Fields makes last request: "I'd like to see Paris before I die—Philadelphia will do"; "My Little Chickadee." (Courtesy of Universal Pictures)

Wyatt Earp, Bat Masterson . . . and now Cuthbert J. Twillie. Fields as the newly appointed sheriff of Greasewood City. (Courtesy of Universal Pictures)

Fields woos Mae West; "My Little Chickadee." (Courtesy of Universal Pictures)

"Anything worth having is worth cheating for," is his perfectly logical retort.

But the town vigilantes have spotted him in his bandit suit. As they march him off for lynching, he pleads his innocence in vain. "I was at a masquerade party," he insists, "impersonating a Ubangi." A huge noose around his neck, Twillie is asked if he has anything to say. "This will be a great lesson to me," he replies, and when asked if he has any last requests, hopefully says, "Yes, I'd like to see Paris before I die." Feeling the noose tighten around his neck he adds hastily, "Philadelphia will do!"

Flowerbelle meanwhile has sought out the real masked bandit and persuaded him to put in an appearance—thus proving Twillie's innocence—and at the same time return all of his ill-gotten loot. Surprisingly, the bandit agrees. His appearance—and escape—prove that Twillie is not an outlaw, and he is released. When all the excitement dies down and the truth of the fake marriage is revealed, Flowerbelle is ardently courted by two suitors—the now reformed saloon-keeper (and masked bandit), and the honest and incorruptible newspaper editor (Dick Foran) who has always worshiped her.

She refuses to commit herself, however, and suggests that since she is available, both men continue to fight over her. As she wiggles upstairs to her boudoir, she meets Twillie on his way down. Unreformed by his brush with death, he is on his way back East to organize his latest confidence scheme—hair-oil wells! Miss West and Fields imitate the other's catch-phrases as they bid each other farewell. And Mae West, who had the opening reel to herself, also wraps up the fadeout gag, the "End" title being superimposed over her swaying derrière.

Nevertheless, "My Little Chickadee" remained indisputably Fields' picture. Even allowing that Mae West was hampered by Code restrictions where Fields was not (a difficulty she had managed to side-step in such immediate post-Code films as "Goin' to Town"), she came off a very second best. However, her presence was surely a box-office asset, and the film—the only really elaborate production among them—was the most profitable of the four starring vehicles that Fields was to make for Universal.

Mr. Egbert Sousé expounds on latest detective methods to pal (Bill Wolf); *"The Bank Dick."* (Courtesy of Universal Pictures)

☞ 16.

The Last Classic

It is unusual indeed for any film craftsman—be he actor, comedian, writer, director or even musical composer—to turn out some of the finest work of his career at the very climax of that career. More commonly one finds that the most flamboyant talents (Orson Welles, Rouben Mamoulian, John Huston, Danny Kaye) do their best film work at the beginning of their careers, when they are unaware of all the rules they are not supposed to break. Or one finds a steady climb to a mid-career high point—as in the films of director John Ford, certainly at his peak in the late thirties and early forties—and thence a gradual decline.

Fields, who broke so many rules, can be said to have broken these as well. His second-from-the-last starring vehicle, 1940's "The Bank Dick," is quite possibly his finest work, and by any standards a lasting classic of screen comedy. Perhaps less disciplined than "It's a Gift," the only other Fields film entitled to stand beside it in full equality, it is also quite different. And it is even less concerned with plot than was usual with Fields, although the tangled threads and multiple characters are interwoven with a dexterity that would have done justice to Dickens or Griffith! It is a kind of Fields mosaic, a summing-up of his life's work, favorite gags and pet peeves, but with a new and mellow warmth that is most endearing. The half-dozen minor plot-lines skip along so nimbly that there is never any time to devote to a routine as carefully worked out as the sleeping-porch episode in "It's a Gift"; yet there is no sense of undue haste either. Somehow one feels that not only did Fields have a thoroughly free hand in its construction, but the final result must have been very much to his liking as well.

For his original story, Fields adopted his most impressive pen-name to date—Mahatma Kane Jeeves. And the extraordinary tale he spins, set in the sleepy little town of Lompoc where all the news, or the lack of it, is dispensed by a newspaper called The Picayune Intelligentsia, was certainly worthy of such a dignified pseudonym.

Fields, long unemployed but of moderately comfortable means, plays Egbert Sousé, care of course being taken to emphasize the all-important accent over the "é." With him lives the Fields family to end them all. Wife Agatha, a crotchety shrew forever clad in shapeless dressing-gown and hair-curlers, whose key aim in life seems to be to prevent Egbert from smoking and drinking, is played by Cora Witherspoon.

His mother, Mrs. Hermisillo Brunch, does little but rock back and forth, grumble, and issue a triumphant "Hah!" every time Egbert is called to account for some minor misdemeanor. Mrs. Brunch is in the capable hands of Jessie Ralph, as expert a harridan as she could be a tear-stained grandmother.

There is an obnoxious brat of a child, of course—Elsie Mae Adele Brunch Sousé, played by Evelyn Del Rio. Father and daughter understand each other rather well; she sneers at him in the street and pelts him with rocks, and when she isn't looking he tries to heave a huge heavy vase at her. There is also the grown-up daughter, Myrtle Sousé, played by Una Merkel. Despite a tendency to dissolve into tears, and oft-stated threats to commit suicide by starving herself to death, she isn't a bad sort in her simple-minded way, and Fields does all that he can to smooth the path of her romance with Og Oggilby, her dim-witted boyfriend (who else but Grady Sutton?). Fairly early in the film, the Sousé fortunes seem to take a turn for the better when a film unit, shooting location scenes in Lompoc, is stalled by the utter inebriation of the director, A. Pismo Clam, played by Jack Norton, the movies' dapper perennial drunk. Clam is walked back and forth across the screen in sobering-up attempts, but to no avail. Not unnaturally the production supervisor comes to the Black Pussy Cat saloon to drown his sorrows and, also not unnaturally, encounters Fields there.

"Would you entertain a proposition to direct this picture?" he asks Fields, who has been regaling him with tales of his experiences with Mack Sennett. As long as he is given the treatment befitting a man of his station, Fields is prepared

Sousé, as pinch-hitter film director, is howled down by derisive small daughter Elsie (Evelyn Del Rio); "The Bank Dick." (Courtesy of Universal Pictures)

to accept—and he is carried on to the location, Indian-rajah style, in a makeshift howdah hastily assembled by the crew. Not too much shooting is actually completed. The matinee-idol leading man (Reed Hadley, before his days of prominence) is wearing top hat and tails; the heroine is a shrimp who comes up to his waist (Fields asks innocently if she is standing in a hole); and neither of them seems quite appropriate to the football scrimmage scene that the script has listed for the Lompoc Main Street location. Fields' expert eye detects what is wrong; he rips out a page or two, hastily devises some new action, and then is toppled from his majestic perch by the arrival of his younger daughter, demanding to be put into the picture. Fortunately, by now the professional director, though still having to be supported by his aides, is considered sufficiently recovered to resume command of the epic.

The basic "plot," however, really gets under way when two bank robbers, Filthy McNasty and Repulsive Rogan, hold up the local bank. By pure chance (and fortuitously without witnesses) one of them stumbles over Fields as he sits reading on a bench, and is knocked cold. With characteristic humility, Fields

Fields' anxious fellow-depositor in "The Bank Dick." (Courtesy of Universal Pictures)

admits his responsibility for the ruffian's capture despite the mighty struggle he put up with an assegai that was this long—no, *this* long—and which has somehow disappeared in the confusion.

Later, Fields finds that the hero's honors which the townspeople want to bestow upon him aren't duplicated in his own home, where the response is one not so much of disbelief as of unconcern. Seeking a little of the respect so long denied him, he strolls in casually with the newspaper account of his heroics rather too obviously displayed under his arm. He murmurs something about capturing the bandit, hoping that he'll be asked to amplify. But wife Agatha is much too busy with her bridge game, and merely snatches the paper and tosses it unread into the fire.

Dismayed but resigned, Fields decides to go up to his room, while mother-in-law's disgusting puffing noises, a finger stuck in her mouth, are an unsubtle reminder to him that he'd better not do any smoking up there. The point is academic anyway; the distracted Fields misses the stairs, and climbs onto a hassock and a bookcase instead. If the family does not appreciate him there are others who do, and he is cheered by the thought of the reward he has been promised by the grateful bank president.

On his way to the bank next morning, feeling thoroughly at peace with the world, he offers his helpful advice to a harassed chauffeur working on a stalled limousine. The advice is definitely not appreciated, and the chauffeur is more than a little surly in refusing Fields' request for a wrench so that he can straighten the whole thing out. But the sweet little old lady sitting patiently in the back of the limousine is grateful for the stranger's consideration and gently reprimands her driver, telling him to let Fields do whatever he can to help.

Murderously, the chauffeur flings the wrench at Fields' head, but Fields catches it deftly, approaches the open motor, studies it for a moment, and makes a single turn of a screw. The entire engine immediately drops into the dust of Main Street. With a sheepish grin of half-hearted apology, Fields takes his leave and resumes his stroll to the bank. (Hours later, when Fields chances to pass that way again, the sweating chauffeur is still trying to repair the damage.)

The bank is not unduly busy, but there appears to be only one teller on duty. As soon as Fields gets to a window and tries to state his business, he is abruptly directed to the next window, or told to stand aside for a moment. After several repetitions of this, Fields becomes a trifle peeved, and as he is turned away yet again, he reacts in mock horror at finding a Negro gentleman standing right behind him. This depositor is quite agitated and wants to draw out his entire account. Reluctant to let the money go, the teller asks him why.

"Well, suh," explains the suspicious one, "every time I comes in here you is wearing a hat, and it looks like you is getting ready to take off!" The teller's explanation that he is wearing a hat because of a head cold obviously does not cut much ice with either the depositor or Fields (whose old aversion to "Ethiopians" seems now to have lost its sting). Fields manages to get in to see the

Fields serves a short stint as a substitute director in "The Bank Dick." (Courtesy of Universal Pictures)

While Fields' attitude toward children mellowed a trifle in his last films, the gag publicity stills didn't. (Courtesy of Universal Pictures)

Fields strikes back against youthful persecutor and mother Jan Duggan; "The Bank Dick." (Courtesy of Universal Pictures)

president, Mr. Skinner, a dapper, pursed-lipped, unemotional smoothie, flawlessly type-cast in the person of Pierre Watkin.

Mr. Skinner is mildly puzzled about some aspects of the capture, particularly the assegai knife. This reminds Fields of a story, and he entertains Mr. Skinner with a melodramatic account of a fight he once had with Major Moe, a colored midget. Major Moe was using an assegai, too, although on second thought Fields recalls, "It wasn't so much a knife as it was a razor." (It troubles no one that an assegai is a spear, not a knife.)

The facts concerning the capture thus successfully obscured, Fields ogles a sexy secretary who wanders in and out, and then settles down to receive his reward. Firstly—and the tone of his voice indicates that this is the greatest honor of all—the president extends a "hearty hand-shake." This consists of Mr. Skinner's fingers barely touching Fields' outstretched palm for a moment—an effect that Fields heightens by going to a split-second freeze-frame. The material rewards are, one, a copy of the bank's calendar, illustrated with an inspiring painting of "Spring in Lompoc," and, two, the offer of a splendid job, that of bank detective, or—as Mr.

Con-man Russell Hicks waits his chance, as Egbert Sousé discusses problems with bartender (Shemp Howard); "The Bank Dick." (Courtesy of Universal Pictures)

Skinner puts it with a mirthless laugh—"in the parlance of the underworld, a bank dick."

The advantages of this are outlined to Fields; it would be easy to reward him by giving him a top executive position, but this is a much greater reward because it will enable him to learn the banking business from the bottom up, and the possibilities are unlimited. Fields somewhat unconvincingly agrees that this is indeed the best of all possible rewards, and adds, "That's all right, I think I can make that," when told that the bank opens at ten in the morning.

Since prospective son-in-law Og works in the bank too, Fields takes Og into his confidence and tells him of the crime-busting methods he plans to utilize, one of which will be a series of master disguises. The first disguise next morning, consisting merely of a moustache, a policeman's uniform and an outsized badge, fools nobody, however.

Deeply conscious of his responsibilities, Fields is taking no chances with potential marauders. Jan Duggan (his old vis-à-vis from "The Old-Fashioned Way") enters with her small son, who is sporting a cowboy outfit and toy gun.

199

Sneaking up on them stealthily, Fields grabs the possibly embryonic bank robber and throttles him. The little boy, finally released, makes fun of Fields by ridiculing his shiny red nose. But the boy's mother chides him for making fun of the misfortunes of others, and adds, "Wouldn't you like to have a large nose like that, all full of nickels?"

The next chunk of substantial plot rears its unlikely head when Fields gravitates back to the Black Pussy Cat cafe again for a "depth bomb." Ordering a glass of water, he washes his fingers in it fastidiously and dries them on a napkin which he rolls into a ball; he tosses it into the air, neatly catches it and kicks it away with his foot, and orders a second glass of water. "Never like to bathe in the same water twice," he explains to his uninterested neighbor, that living corpse William Wolf who joined Fields in propping up so many bars in so many movies.

Enter J. Frothingham Waterbury, the most obvious of con-men, flawlessly attired in white panama hat and expensive clothes, and with an unbeatable line in slick patter. He lets his presence sink in for a moment, wiping the perspiration from his brow to indicate the desperate predicament he is in. "Gosh!" he suddenly explodes, and then is instantly and abjectly apologetic for his profanity. Fields assures him that it's all right.

This gives Waterbury the in he needs. Fields is obviously an intelligent man; perhaps he can be the one to benefit from Waterbury's sad personal misfortune. He has to raise money; he would almost rather sell his grandmother's old paisley shawl than this (Fields nods his realization of what a sacrifice that would be), but it has to be done. Fields can have Waterbury's stocks in the Beefsteak Mine, and all for a few hundred dollars.

Waterbury paints a magnificent word picture of the luxuries that will soon be his. Fields will sit in his country estate, and in the terraced gardens a river of beer will run past his feet. Every so often fleets of armored trucks will drive up to deposit strongboxes full of cash, and his only exertion will be to sign his name when the guard gives him a receipt and says "Sign here."

It is this last inducement that convinces Fields of the monetary advantages of the scheme.

"I'll have a fountain pen by then," he nods in assent.

Fields closes the deal with Waterbury, but has to get the cash first—and what better source than Og, who works in the bank? Fields explains to the very dubious Og that taking the money from the bank won't be stealing—he'll be replacing it almost immediately—and think of what it will mean to him. Now he can get married right away, and live in a big country place with his grandmother's paisley shawl running through it.

The items discussed get a little jumbled in Fields' excited mind, but his enthusiasm is unmistakable, and Og is almost won over. Fields presses his advantage. "Don't be a fuddie-duddie, don't be a moon-calf, don't be a jabbernowl—you don't want to be any of those, do you?"

To prove how right he is, Fields calls again upon the voice of experience and relates the impressive story of Uncle Ichabod, who likewise was faced with the need to make an instant decision and acted without hesitation. It seems that Ichabod was adrift in a runaway balloon without a parachute, and he leaped over the side, taking a chance that he would land on a haystack. Fields comes to the end of his narrative, pridefully sure that he has proved his point.

"Did he make it?" queries the still undecided Og.

"No," admits Fields reluctantly, "but that just proves my point. Had he been a younger man he probably would have!"

Unconvinced, but with greed outweighing caution, Og agrees to "borrow" the money, and the deal is made. The Beefsteak shares and a life of ease will be theirs.

The next morning, however, their world crumbles hopelessly when the door of the bank opens and in walks pompous, prissy, incorruptible J. Pinkerton Snoopington, the bank examiner. Snoopington is played by Franklin Pangborn, he of the pussy-cat face, expert at playing either ultra-dignified VIPs, fey and effeminate dress designers, hotel managers or theatrical impresarios. Invaluable in comedy of the thirties and forties, he frequently was put to brilliant use by Lubitsch, Preston Sturges and by Fields, and had appeared (though less effectively) in many of the early sound shorts produced by Sennett. Accosting Snoopington before he has had time to make his presence known, Fields tells him a lying rigamarole about the bank president's being away, and somehow lures him into a quick tour of Lompoc. It is Fields' intention to get Snoopington into a drunken stupor, but obviously this isn't going to be easy. He is a man of impossibly adhered-to virtues, refuses to take a drink, and will not even take advantage of Fields' generous offer to weigh himself for nothing at a store where Fields has considerable influence with the proprietor.

Quite by accident, their steps stray by the Black Pussy Cat cafe, and Fields suggests that they stop in for a moment for a drink of fruit juice. Against his better judgment, Snoopington agrees, but when they sit down by a window he asks if the shade can be pulled. "Oh, sure," agrees Fields amiably; "you can pull anything you like in here. It's a regular joint." After some pointed references to the bartender about the whereabouts of Michael Finn, Snoopington is served with not one but two savagely spiked drinks. Before long he is such a quivering mass of agonised nausea that any thought of work is out of the question, and he asks to be taken to his hotel.

As they enter the lobby, Fields chidingly suggests that he pull himself together a bit, as this is a respectable hotel. They disappear up the stairs. Moments later Fields rushes down in a frenzy, sprints out into the street, and then leads Snoopington back into the lobby again, his even more dazed and battered look and the several layers of dust on his clothes testifying to the effects of his (off-screen) fall from a second-story window.

Snoopington is safely bedded, and lies there moaning as Fields kindly says that maybe what he needs is a good meal to perk him up. Some pork chops per-

A *law officer has many things on his mind;* "*The Bank Dick.*" (Courtesy of Universal Pictures)

". . . *Your grandmother's paisley shawl running through the estate . . .*" Bank clerk Grady Sutton *listens to build-up for misappropriation of funds;* "*The Bank Dick.*" (Courtesy of Universal Pictures)

haps, with plenty of onions and grease. Snoopington heaves visibly, and assures his well-meaning friend that food is not uppermost in his mind at this time, but that he does need a doctor.

Obligingly Fields calls Dr. Stall, an aggressive, no-nonsense little man who is engaged in giving the emaciated Bill Wolf a check-up. Wolf is stripped to the waist and looking ready to fall into an open grave at any moment. The doctor's diagnosis is brisk and succinct. The patient must cut out all health foods, and get plenty of rest. "That'll be ten dollars; the nurse will return your clothes with your receipt."

Doc Stall bursts into Snoopington's room of pain with a cheerful disregard for his patient and a comradely greeting for his old pal Fields. Business isn't too bad, he admits cheerfully, but nothing like the good old days; they don't have those nice profitable whooping cough epidemics any more. Grudgingly he turns his attention to Snoopington, gives him the most cursory of examinations, orders him to cut out all physical exercise, and then produces a jar filled with noxious-looking white pills—although "pills" is rather an understatement, since they are fully the size of ping-pong balls.

Once the doctor has left, Fields again returns to the subject of food. This time his description of the kind of meal that Snoopington needs to pep him up is so vivid and so often punctuated with references to fried and greasy items that Snoopington bounds out of bed and barely makes it to the bathroom before disaster overtakes him. "Poor fellow's had nothing to eat!" Fields clucks sympathetically as the scene fades.

Alas! however, Snoopington reappears at the bank the next morning, white around the gills but determined to let nothing interfere with the loyal observance of his sacred duty. Fields somehow maneuvers him close to a letter press and squeezes the mechanism down on Snoopington's hand with a bone-shattering crunch.

"What a pity," comments Fields. "That'll interfere with your writing, won't it?"

Acidly, Snoopington says that he is ambidextrous, whereupon he drops his glasses. "Can't see a thing without them!" he mutters, groping for them. Fields rushes to his aid, in the process managing to crush the glasses beneath the heel of his shoe. Sorrowfully, he holds up the completely shattered spectacles, but this device does not work either. Snoopington, who by now is entertaining a dawning suspicion that perhaps there is a plot afoot to keep him from checking the books, has a whole brief-case full of replacement spectacles.

Meantime, salvation is almost at hand. The Beefsteak Mine shares have proven to be worth a fortune, and J. Frothingham Waterbury, feigning sorrow at having unwittingly bilked a trusting friend, seeks out Fields to buy them back. As Fields is about to tell Og the good news, Repulsive Rogan puts in a return engagement, and robs the bank once more. This time using Fields as a shield and driver, he makes his getaway in a fast car.

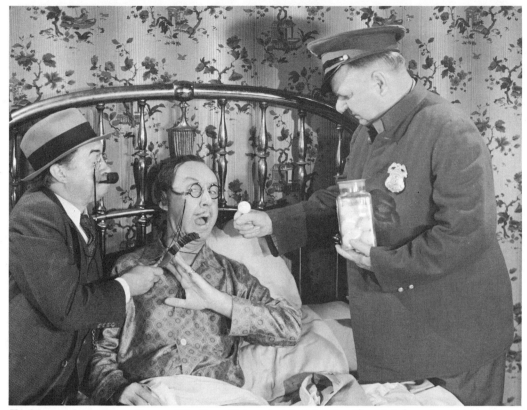

Fields and doctor chum (Harlan Briggs) minister to the stricken bank examiner (Franklin Pangborn); "The Bank Dick." (Courtesy of Universal Pictures)

The local constabulary follow in a second car and the bank president in a third—accompanied by a representative from the movie company who has arrived in town just in time for the excitement. The chase that follows is a fast *mélange* of screeching tires, near-collisions, continuous sight gags (many of them directly traceable to such Sennett slapstickers of the twenties as "Lizzies of the Field") and expertly precise stunt work, all accompanied by the comments of Fields, who seeks to distract the attention of his captor by commenting fruitily on the beauties of the rapidly passing countryside.

The rear wheel begins to slide off its axle, but Fields, unruffled, merely remarks, "That could be serious!"

The three cars careen through the country lanes and up steep mountain roads, doubling back, circling each other in meticulously timed stunt scenes, until Repulsive Rogan is knocked senseless by the bough of a tree, and Fields brings the car to a halt on the very brink of a precipice.

Once more he is the hero of the hour and the recipient of a second hearty hand-shake from Mr. Skinner. The bank's money is recovered, and the unsus-

*Elsie watches cynically as Sousé takes leave of older daughter (Una Merkel).
Of course he's not going to the Black Pussy Cat cafe! "The Bank Dick." (Courtesy
of Universal Pictures)*

pected value of the Beefsteak shares augurs well for Fields' rivers of beer and paisley shawls, as well as Og's marital happiness. Finally, the studio executive brings Fields not only a million-dollar contract to produce and direct a new movie, but also a large check for the brilliant script that he concocted earlier in the streets of Lompoc.

Universal executives may have felt a trifle chagrined at this final dig, for the farrago of a script that he had constructed was as wild and as brief as the two-page story-lines that he sold as "scripts" to Universal and for which he commonly demanded payment running into thousands of dollars.

Life in the Sousé household is now totally reshaped, and Fields emerges finally and positively as master of the house. Not given to recriminations, he accepts his new status with dignity, never over-playing his hand as wife and mother-in-law now fawn on him and cater to his every whim, practically forcing "just one more Baba au Rhum" on him before he leaves for the day's business.

He has a cutaway coat and spats now, and a butler who gently advises him that a top hat is perhaps more suitable than the African safari helmet that he first tries on. A flourish of the cane once more hoists his top hat out of reach just as it is about to be placed on his head. Walking happily into his spacious gardens, he pauses to shoot a tin can out of his way with a deft kick, and then, spying his favorite bartender en route to the Black Pussy Cat cafe, instinctively quickens his step and gives chase.

This whole epilogue, played against an unobtrusive arrangement of "There's No Place Like Home," has a curious kind of warmth and melancholy to it. It is as though Fields, like Egbert Sousé, has finally found both peace and satisfaction, and, having paid off all his old scores, is happy to call it quits.

There is an emotional quality to the scene not unlike that moment when William S. Hart, having bade farewell to his fans and literally delivered his own obituary (in the special introduction which was filmed for the 1939 reissue of his silent classic, "Tumbleweeds"), turns his back on the camera for the last time and walks dramatically into the sunset.

A handful of Fields films still lay ahead, but "The Bank Dick" was the true apex of his career. He had never made, nor would he make, a funnier film, nor would he ever top the poignancy of this moment when he, too, in effect, said goodbye.

Egbert (W. C. Fields) incurs the displeasure of his butler (Joe North) when he calls for his sun helmet to wear with his morning suit.

Fields prepares to dive from plane, without parachute, after lost bottle; "Never Give a Sucker an Even Break." (Courtesy of Universal Pictures)

☞ 17.

Swan Song

At any other time, "Never Give a Sucker an Even Break" might well have been regarded as a minor masterpiece. But coming right after the well-nigh perfect "The Bank Dick," "Never Give a Sucker an Even Break" (made in 1941, Fields' last starring vehicle), good as it is, seemed self-indulgent and erratic. Had it gone into release a few months later, after another Universal film, "Hellza-poppin'," had established a precedent for wildly lunatic comedy, it might have fared better. But the truly insane comedy—the films of Olsen and Johnson and the Marx Brothers—which have movies within movies and characters that frequently leave the action to converse with the audience, had no place in the world of W. C. Fields, which for all of its bizzare and whimsical quality was still a fairly realistic world.

In "Hellzapoppin'," it was the gags themselves, and the piling of insanity upon insanity, that provided the humor. Olsen and Johnson were merely instruments for the unleashing of those gags, and they were never funny in themselves. In any Fields film, he was always the pivot around which the gags revolved, and indeed many of the gags would not have worked at all with any other comedian. Furthermore, regardless of rambling story-lines, there was an indisputable discipline to all of the better Fields vehicles; either the discipline of the experienced vaudevillian, as in "The Man on the Flying Trapeze," or that of the experienced film-maker, so notably demonstrated in "The Bank Dick." "Never Give a Sucker an Even Break" had neither discipline nor even consistency. Fields, who hated any of the formula methods of making movies, gave in to formula by halting his production every now and then so that the youthful star Gloria Jean could sing.

Even allowing for the story premise that most of the film turns out to be merely a fabrication of his imagination, part of a film scenario that Fields is trying to sell to the Esoteric Studios, there are so many holes in the picture and so many loose ends—many of which appear to be created by last-minute cuts —that the "official" synopsis of "Never Give a Sucker an Even Break" bears almost no resemblance to the film. It is almost as though Fields, pleased by the success which rewarded his unfettered imagination on "The Bank Dick," here decided to go it one better by striving for the bizarre instead of letting it seem to flow naturally from a basic character and situation.

Individual components of "Never Give a Sucker an Even Break" show Fields at his very best, but there is no cohesion to them and the film is spotty in its comedy, jerky in its construction. In later years, its very untidiness came to be regarded as a virtue by some of the higher-browed critics, who professed to see in it a form of "rebellion" against the Hollywood system. Along with "The Bank Dick," it came to be accepted as a regular repeater at the *chi-chi* little art houses that looked down their noses at it when it appeared in the forties. However, perhaps the shortcomings of "Never Give a Sucker an Even Break" are emphasized because of its immediate proximity to "The Bank Dick"; though certainly not one of Fields' top half-dozen works, it is still not a film to be dismissed lightly.

Though it includes such flights of fancy as Fields leaping from an airplane to retrieve his beloved bottle, it is at its funniest when at its simplest. Especially delightful are Fields' tiltings with that female mountain of flesh Jody Gilbert, playing the waitress in a diner. "I didn't make disparaging remarks about your steak," he tells her in a hurt tone. "I merely said that I hadn't seen that old horse that you used to keep outside around here lately!" Departing after his meal, he accidentally tears his straw hat apart on the hat-rack and, leaving it hanging there, calmly takes the hat next to it. But before he can get away, its owner, who has witnessed the substitution, stops him with a threatening "That's my hat you've got there!" Fields pauses, innocently inspects the hat, which is not at all like his own, and comes to the gradual conclusion that perhaps he has made a mistake.

"So it is, so it is," he purrs, and apologizes for a mistake which he implies was perfectly natural.

Taking his young niece Gloria with him to Mexico, where he plans to make

The death of Madame Gorgeous (Ann Nagel), trapeze-artist mother of Gloria Jean; a plot element entirely deleted from the final cut of "Never Give a Sucker an Even Break." (Courtesy of Universal Pictures)

a fortune selling nutmegs to members of a Russian colony, he contrives to have the plane peopled by a number of diverse comedy types (including silly-ass Englishman Claude Allister) who provide outlets for many favorite one-liners and gag situations. Sitting by an open window in the observation platform (the separately seen sections of this airplane would combine into a very unwieldy whole!) he accidentally nudges his bottle over the side and frantically dives after it. He lands on the mountain-top retreat of the eccentric Mrs. Hemogloben (Margaret Dumont), whose lovely and virginal daughter Ouliotta (Susan Miller) is only too happy to be introduced to a kissing game.

As the first man she has ever met, Fields realizes he is on to a good thing, but his romantic kisses (which he describes as a popular game called "squidgum") are interrupted when Ouliotta sees mother approaching. There is a throat-rumbling bark and Mrs. Hemogloben enters in a Lady MacBeth black flowing robe, accompanied by a fanged mastiff. It is never clearly established whether the bark emanated from the dog or Mrs. Hemogloben. In any event, she has romantic inclinations of her own toward Fields, but her ardor, not to mention her

Fields chooses between his *hat, and a hat in one piece; "Never Give a Sucker an Even Break."* (Courtesy of Universal Pictures)

dragon-like face and Amazonian proportions, terrifies Fields, who beats a tactical retreat.

Fortunately there is an improvised elevator affixed to the mountainside— a balloon basket raised and lowered by a winch—and he soon has made a lightning descent to civilization. Entirely by coincidence, he finds himself in the Russian colony in Mexico where he was heading before his spectacular dive from the plane. A business rival, Leon Errol, has beaten him to the punch and already is entrenched in the nutmeg-selling industry. Gloria Jean reappears from nowhere, in the company of a band of strolling gypsy musicians.

Fields and Errol both overhear remarks to the effect that Mrs. Hemogloben is fabulously wealthy, and decide to win her hand. Fields and Gloria get to the basket first, and thus have a head-start, especially as Errol, climbing the mountainside in a Tyrolean outfit, is further delayed by a chance encounter with a giant gorilla. (Gorillas not being natural denizens of Mexico or of mountainous terrains, one suspects that this sequence was inspired by a similarly unlikely Laurel

"Never Give a Sucker an Even Break"; a repeat of the sleeping berth sequence from "The Old-Fashioned Way." (Courtesy of Universal Pictures)

and Hardy versus giant gorilla encounter in "Swiss Miss" three or four years earlier.)

Over the protestations of Gloria, who hates to see her uncle marrying for money, Fields' hand-kissing gallantry and florid oratory soon win the heart of Mrs. Hemogloben, and when Errol finally arrives to launch his campaign, Fields disposes of his unwanted rival by tossing him off the mountain.

Even allowing for a general unhealthiness which occasionally pervaded Fields' work, there is a distinctly unsatisfying and distasteful air to both of the lengthy sequences atop the Hemogloben mountain. The sets have a seedy and tatty look to them; the unsympathetic quality of the Fields character quite swamps the considerable fun he is able to extract from the situations; and the usually magnificent Margaret Dumont plays in an oddly humorless way. It all has the look of a rather low-grade burlesque act, as though it were the prelude to either a strip or a prolonged dirty joke, and, although neither of those eventualities come to pass, the bad taste remains.

At the mountain retreat of rich, eccentric Mrs. Hemogloben; "Never Give a Sucker an Even Break." (Courtesy of Universal Pictures)

Gloria finally persuades her uncle that the marriage would be a mistake, and once more they resort to that potential death-trap of a basket. Spilled out at the bottom, Fields is knocked almost senseless by a falling rock. "Are you hurt?" inquires Gloria. "No," replies Fields, keeping his temper and sarcasm admirably under control, "how could a rock falling ten thousand feet possibly hurt anyone?"

At this point, the narrative switches to the Esoteric Studio office of movie executive Franklin Pangborn, who, like the audience, can no longer remember where reality ended and Fields' proposed movie script began, and throws the impossible person out. Fields now wants to take off for parts unknown and leave Gloria in school, but she is having none of this. "Do you want to grow up and be dumb like ZaSu Pitts?" he asks her.

But he gives in, gives her a dollar—"Buy yourself several outfits"—and waits for her in his car outside a department store. Two policemen in their radio patrol car are listening to the reports of crimes throughout the city. ". . .

Fields takes the elevator down from Mrs. Hemogloben's hideaway; "Never Give a Sucker an Even Break." (Courtesy of Universal Pictures)

the bandit got away with ten thousand dollars . . . that is all," drones the voice over the radio.

"That is all?" queries Fields indignantly. "It ain't hay, is it?"

Next over the radio comes the description of a colorful-sounding "wanted" man who has apple-red cheeks, mutton-chop sideburns and other similarly appetizing characteristics. "Sounds like a full-course luncheon!" Fields comments jovially, as the harassed policemen vainly try to concentrate on their orders.

Inside the store, an unusually plump lady who is buying baby clothes suddenly realizes that she is late; she has only time to deliver the clothes to a maternity hospital and catch her plane out of town. In great agitation, she runs out of the store seeking a taxi, but none is to be found. "Can I be of any assistance?" Fields offers generously. Gratefully, the lady accepts, and asks him to rush her to the maternity hospital.

Jumping to the obvious conclusion, he roars away at top speed. His scared passenger tries to attract his attention and get him to slow down, but he mistakes

The reward of total unselfishness; "Never Give a Sucker an Even Break." (Courtesy of Universal Pictures)

her concern as a sign that even greater speed is needed, and jams the accelerator down to the floor-boards. The poor lady swoons in fright, and Fields, glancing back, sees his passenger unconscious, her body jostled back and forth in the speeding car, and apparently in the throes of early labor! Fields never needed wild slapstick chases to conclude his films, but the chase at the end of "Never Give a Sucker an Even Break" is a masterpiece of its kind, quite the finest such chase ever created in the sound cinema.

Staged by second-unit director Ralph Ceder, and employing the services of some of Hollywood's top stunt men (including David Sharpe, who reappears throughout the chase in different guises as victims of the various speeding cars), the sequence is shot largely on the Hollywood Freeway. Traffic problems alone would prevent such a sequence being filmed today, and even in the forties it was a marvel of precision and vehicular choreography.

It dovetails three levels of humor: Fields' caustic comments at the progression of disasters that befall him; the individual sight gags as between pedestrian and car; the much larger-scale action involving cops on motorcycles; the mass destruction of other cars that inconsiderately get in the way; and finally an involvement with a fire-engine which somehow hooks its ladder into the roof of Fields' car. The fire engine takes the road to the left, Fields the uphill drive to the right, the ladder between them serving as a kind of umbilical cord until Fields' car is hoisted into mid-air, dumped with a crash back on the highway, spun around in circles as the fire engine makes some lightning turns, and finally deposited as a heap of junk beside the "Quiet!" sign outside the maternity hospital. His hapless passenger is seized and wheeled into the delivery room, where fortunately she recovers consciousness just in time.

Despite its lack of neatness, "Never Give a Sucker an Even Break" was a delight for the Fields fanciers—though calculated to alienate any who hadn't yet made up their minds about him. Still, even the doubters must have been delighted by the sight of Fields elegantly blowing the froth off an ice-cream soda, or earnestly assuring his niece that what he is drinking is only goat's milk. ("What *kind* of goat's milk, Uncle?" "Er—*nanny* goat's milk, dear.") And the final chase, running for almost a full reel, was such a marvel of its kind, and such a welcome reminder of the then almost forgotten art of sight-gag comedy, that many earlier ineptitudes were forgotten in gales of audience laughter.

Britain, incidentally, which had changed the title "The Bank Dick" to the more proper "The Bank Detective," likewise gave "Never Give a Sucker an Even Break" a more prosaic sobriquet. It emerged as "What a Man!" (a nondescript title that had been used on at least two or three other occasions) and even those critics who weren't devotees of Fields protested this unimaginative blasphemy.

Fields in Chinese hat; late portrait, not retouched. (Courtesy of Universal Pictures)

 **18.**

The Final Encores

The last four W. C. Fields films—none of them starring vehicles—were made over a three-year period ending in late 1944. Now seriously ill, the strain of another full-length feature would have been too much for him, and too much of a risk for a studio which undoubtedly could no longer get insurance to cover them should his illness, or death, force them to close down an unfinished picture. Working with Fields in guest-spots became a problem toward the end, when his undampened spirits could not prevent signs of age and illness from spreading over his face. The makeup men worked minor miracles as it was; unretouched publicity stills of Fields at this time show him looking far older than he ever appeared in a movie.

One of Fields' directors in these last years recalls that his physical condition was so appallingly weak that blood frequently would appear through the pores of his face, necessitating immediate medical attention and further drastic makeup camouflage. Nevertheless, there was no apparent lessening in his ability to rack up laughs, and his final movie appearances, while perhaps unworthy of his professional standing, maintained his own high personal standards. There was none of the gradual decline into cheaper productions that marked the final pictures of such other

219

Fields in Mexican hat; late portrait, not retouched. (Courtesy of Universal Pictures)

Fields juggles a pool ball on a cue for A. Edward (Eddie) Sutherland, director of the all-star "Follow the Boys." (Courtesy of Universal Pictures)

Fields signs autographs for servicemen visiting the set of "Follow the Boys." (Courtesy of Universal Pictures)

All other remedies failing, Fields tries for hair of dog. (Gag publicity still) (Courtesy of Universal Pictures)

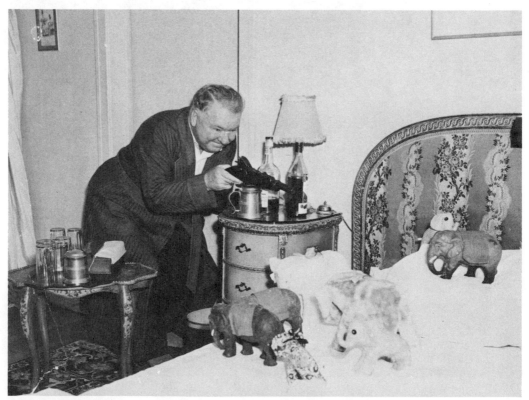

Mr. Fields, beset by small hangover animals, fights back. (Courtesy of Universal Pictures)

comedians as Laurel and Hardy, the Marx Brothers or Abbott and Costello. "Never Give a Sucker an Even Break," far from his best movie but a thoroughly typical and wholly personal one, can be regarded as his official farewell to the screen, the subsequent guest segments to be seen as curtain calls to an audience that was reluctant to let him go.

What was probably the best of these curtain calls, an entire Fields sequence in the 1942 "Tales of Manhattan," has never been seen by the public. It was deleted at the last minute as being the easiest to cut, and possibly because it lacked the sophistication of the rest of the film. The format of "Tales of Manhattan" was not unlike that of "If I Had a Million"; unrelated stories covering drama and comedy and providing showcases for a number of top names were linked by a tuxedo and its adventures as it passed from hand to hand.

A sumptuously staged production, interestingly directed by Julien Duvivier and featuring some of Richard Day's most highly stylized sets, a fatal mistake was made in putting its very best episode at the head of the film. The opening story with Charles Boyer, Rita Hayworth and Thomas Mitchell was not only by far the best written and best acted (a triangle situation with a melodramatic theatrical background), but the only one to deliver a genuine O. Henry "punch" for its climax. Thereafter the picture became too brittle and self-consciously clever for its own good.

The Ginger Rogers-Henry Fonda episode, a sophisticated marital farce, was noisy, labored and over-talkative. The Edward G. Robinson episode—he played a down-and-out drunkard who used the tuxedo in order to attend a class reunion of his old law school—was partly saved by Robinson's fine performance, but otherwise weakened by excessive sentiment and the totally illogical behavior of almost everyone concerned.

The Fields sequence was spotted next, a two-reel comedy vignette in which Fields, aided by Margaret Dumont and other familiar faces from his comedy past, played a lecturer at a fund-raising charity function. It could have come at the right time to rescue the film from the bathos of the previous story and from the unfunny Rogers-Fonda episode. However, if it was as funny as one assumes any such sequence with Fields must be, it could well have upset what equilibrium the film had, and rendered the already thin climactic sequence downright intolerable.

As it stands, the charity social serves only as an unseen off-screen device; crooks who have held up the party stuff the stolen money in the tail coat and make their escape. Later one of them tosses the coat from an airplane, forgetting that the money is still in it, and it floats down on to an impoverished Negro community. The money is divided evenly among the inhabitants, who assume that it is a direct answer to their prayers; the now tattered coat ends by decorating a scarecrow. Although visually interesting because of its lighting and stylized sets, this climactic episode is not only maudlin in the extreme, but very dated today because of the blatant Uncle Tomism in the condescending treatment of the Negroes (Paul Robeson, Ethel Waters and Eddie Anderson have the key roles), and because of the curiously Communistic slogans put into their mouths.

Presumably the missing Fields sequence still reposes in the Fox vaults and one day may see the light of day, just as the Fred Allen "Ransom of Red Chief" episode, originally excised from "O. Henry's Full House," finally was released.

"Follow the Boys" (Universal, 1944) was one of the many well-intentioned wartime splurges into patriotism which got by on the nationalistic fervor of the times, and by the incredibly uncritical acceptance of almost any kind of song-and-dance or comedy show. Its plot was a hackneyed and sentimental show-business saga of vaudeville stars George Raft and Vera Zorina who drift apart when he lets a Hollywood career go to his head. It doesn't even miss the oldest trick of all—when the wife throws away an air-tight reunion by refusing to tell her husband that he is about to become a father.

Ultimately he gives his life doing war work; he is torpedoed at sea while organizing troop entertainment. His wife, who now understands him at last, decides to carry on his efforts.

A major portion of the film is devoted to various wartime shows given for the troops, thus allowing a collection of guest stars to do their specialties. The back-slapping and mutual admiration which take place between stars and studio executives quickly reaches the point of nausea, but fortunately it is so ineptly written in the attempt to dispense credit and good will as promiscuously as possible that it is at least unintentionally amusing.

In later years many of the performers must have winced at the saccharine artificiality of it all—especially the Delta Rhythm Boys, delivering a song on "Democracy" and "Racial Equality" in a phonied-up studio exterior that is allegedly Guadalcanal, and Jeanette MacDonald, singing to some of the most inept back-projected footage of a troop audience ever perpetrated. Orson Welles and Marlene Dietrich managed to rise above it to a degree, and Fields effortlessly walked away with the whole show.

Ambling into a troop canteen, he is asked to do his old pool-hall routine, and, with his full bag of tricks, including some minor juggling, the chomped cigar and the hat on the billiard-cue, he responds amiably enough. His old sidekick William Wolf is on hand for nostalgia too. It is a weary and mechanical effort; Fields keeps his wonderful ad-libs to a minimum, concentrates on the job in hand, and performs as though he is aware that this may well be the last time his celebrated routines will be caught on film. But if no longer inspired, he was the highlight of a film that needed far more—indeed the appalling mediocrity of the rest of the movie made Fields' expert professionalism stand out in sharp relief. It was his last association with director Eddie Sutherland.

"Song of the Open Road" (directed by S. Sylvan Simon for United Artists release in 1944) was backed by an extensive publicity campaign to sell its new singing child

Here and on the following pages are typically bizarre publicity shots from the mid-thirties. (Courtesy of Paramount Pictures)

star, Jane Powell, and because the advertising guns that heralded it were so over-powering, critical and audience response was mild. Actually it was a charming little film in its own naive way, dealing with runaway movie star Jane Powell who joins a group of CCC (Civilian Conservation Corps) fruit pickers. Her well-meaning efforts to help them, and her Hollywood-engendered belief that her money can buy anything, soon make her a social leper among the fruit pickers.

In the climax, the tomato crop threatened with destruction, Jane comes through true-blue by bringing her Hollywood pals to put on a show and persuading everybody to pitch in and take part. Her Hollywood cronies were on a surprisingly low social and talent echelon for a star of her alleged magnitude, but at least they included Fields and Charlie McCarthy—plus, of course, Edgar Bergen. The Fields-McCarthy exchanges were desultory at best, and Fields' solicitude toward young

Miss Powell was very much at odds with his carefully nurtured image, but he expertly provided a few laughs and added an element of real showmanship to a film that was otherwise on the quiet side.

Fields had more to do in his final film, "Sensations of 1945" (produced and directed by Andrew Stone, also for United Artists release in 1944), but his guest spot lacked pace and sparkle. His comedy skit with a pretty girl (Louise Currie) in a railway coach looked as though it might have been adapted from a Fields sketch from years back, but with all the humor carefully milked out of it.

Fields was an amusing sight as always in his huge fur coat from the twenties and a dapper straw hat, but his lines were so unfunny that even he couldn't do much with them, and the whole skit wandered along without point until it came to a halt without climax.

It is a pity that this piece of film should turn out to be Fields' final contribution to any of the entertainment media, but it was not quite bad enough, nor the film important enough, for it to matter very much. Dancing star Eleanor Powell—absent from the screen for several years—was in good form and made a welcome return, but the other guest stars, from Sophie Tucker to the bands of Cab Calloway and Woody Herman, were as ill-served as Fields.

As had been the case with "Follow the Boys," however, a definite market existed at the time for this kind of film. Critics approached it with a blind eye, giving it far more applause than it warranted, and audiences generally were pleased. It served its purpose then, and has been properly forgotten ever since.

Fields was sixty-five when he made his last movie. He was tired and very ill, and he knew it. His fingers were stiff and often painful, ruling out the possibility of performing his juggling, poolroom and other routines again, for Fields was proud of his dexterity and would never settle for second-best. Still not admitting that he had made his last movie, he solicited more offers—but none came. A liver ailment and a weakened heart were added to other maladies, and even a now sharply reduced alcoholic intake was of no help to his battered and bruised constitution.

Death finally came to him late in 1946, on the morning of that particular day of the year that he had so consistently hated and cursed because it denoted generosity, good-will, sentimentality and the spending of money on others—Christmas Day.

It is now more than twenty years since Fields died, and almost a quarter of a century since those days in the early forties when Fields and director Preston Sturges (not together, more's the pity) between them rescued and revitalized the whole field of comedy film. Since Sturges worked so felicitously with Harold Lloyd in "Mad Wednesday," one can only conjecture as to the riotous comedy that might have resulted had he and Fields teamed up, even so late in Fields' life. Fields died; Preston Sturges' years of glory were brief, and now he too is dead. Comedy virtually disappeared for a while, and except for its re-emergence as a valuable box-office commodity, nothing really new has happened to make us laugh since then.

The popular Doris Day-Rock Hudson-Cary Grant comedies have been pleasant enough, but are merely re-shufflings of successful formulas. Comedy "spectaculars," such as "It's a Mad Mad Mad Mad World" and "The Great Race," have paid lip service to the earlier comedies and their sight gags, but in trying to "improve" on them and "expand" them, the result has been to over-produce them into marathon bores. Even so highly acclaimed a talent as Dick Lester, director of "The

Knack," "Help!" and "A Funny Thing Happened on the Way to the Forum," has merely been using a combination of styles, predominantly Sennett, which already are showing signs of spectacularly diminishing returns.

Perhaps the only genuinely funny and original comedies of recent years have been those two essays in black humor, "Dr. Strangelove" (which will surely develop into a permanent classic) and the less successful but still interesting "The Loved One." For the rest, a significant development has been the resurgence of audience interest in the great sight-gag and star-vehicle comedies of the twenties and thirties— an interest supported by the availability of many of these films, thanks to television, art houses and film archives.

At first, the Marx Brothers held sole sway over the cultist revivals; now the appeal has become much broader, transcending the specialist cults and the followers of "camp" (a meaningless, lazy and disfiguring term, happily now heading back to obscurity). The popularity of the Marx Brothers remains undimmed, but they have been joined by Laurel and Hardy, Buster Keaton, Mae West and Fields in forming a kind of classic stock company of humorists who should be immune to the ravages of time, morals and fashions. Quite possibly Keaton will always seem the freshest and wittiest of the clowns, and probably Laurel and Hardy will always garner the most laughs in a given reel.

But Fields will almost certainly emerge (if he has not already) as the funniest natural comedian of them all. Laurel and Hardy needed neither props nor situations to get laughs; they could stand on a bare stage, if necessary, and with the subtlety of their facial pantomime, or the inflection of a word or two, create gales of laughter. But even with the apparent ease of their style, one knew that they were working for their laughs, relying on timing, anticipation, audience familiarity with their methods.

Fields, conversely, never seemed to work for his laughs. Indeed, he appeared to ward them off, as though his situation were too pitiful to generate laughter. His best gag lines were usually delivered as thrown-away mumbles and his films nearly always strolled into their "End" title on a note of quiet anti-climax.

There is always something funny—often hilariously so—in the most depressing drudgeries and most saddening tragedies of everyday life. If there were not, and we were unable to see it, life would be hardly worthwhile. Fields made us see it. In laughing at him, we were laughing at life. Thus he didn't have to force our laughter, and we laughed because we wanted to laugh. This eloquent gift was unique unto him, shared by no other comedian. We laughed at the others because they were brilliant or inventive or because we actually came to love them; Fields was brilliant and inventive too, but mostly it was quite enough that he was Bill Fields.